"Completely and totally unwittingly, Paul Koehorst and Jacob Lentz have written perhaps the most important new business book since *Who Moved My Cheese?* and *The One Minute Manager*. *There's No I in Office* can save you from the situation in which people often find themselves when they work for me: getting fired. I can honestly say that, most often, those I sent packing had no rapport with me. If I saw them, they would avert their eyes at all costs. Unsure what to say, they said nothing, and I felt no guilt when I had to let them go. This book puts an end to all of that. Had they read it, hundreds of people whom I fired could have connected with me in a totally unmeaningful and superfluous way and AVOIDED THE AXE!"

**—Jim Cramer**, host of *Mad Money with Jim Cramer*

"I don't even have coworkers, but this book made me want to get some so that I could totally blow them off."

**—Steve Agee**, gay guy "Steve" on
*The Sarah Silverman Program*

"Having 'worked' with Jake and Paul, I can attest that both are masters of office politics. While others struggle to get ahead through tireless effort, these two heroes prove that a well-turned phrase to the right executive trumps doing anything that's actually constructive. In fact, it's the height of irony that the writing of this book represents the first actual 'work' I've seen either do."

**—Dave Dameshek**, 710 ESPN

"If Brian Dunkleman had read this book, Ryan Seacrest would be the one doing *Celebrity Fit Club*. Don't let the same thing happen to you. Buy it, read it, use it. Then watch in amazement as your undeserved success in the workplace arrives."

**—Chris Ayres**, author of *War Reporting for Cowards*

# THERE'S NO I IN OFFICE

**4293 Meaningless Phrases**
to Keep Your Coworkers Smiling
While Avoiding Actual Conversation

Jacob Lentz & Paul Koehorst

Ulysses Press

Text Copyright © 2009 Jacob Lentz and Paul Koehorst. Design Copyright © 2009 Ulysses Press and its licensors. All rights reserved under International and Pan-American Copyright Conventions, including the right to reproduce this book or portions thereof in any form whatsoever, except for use by a reviewer in connection with a review.

Published by:
Ulysses Press
P.O. Box 3440
Berkeley, CA 94703
www.ulyssespress.com

ISBN: 978-1-56975-701-7
Library of Congress Control Number: 2008907001

Printed in the U.S. by Bang Printing

10 9 8 7 6 5 4 3 2 1

Acquisitions Editor: Nicholas Denton-Brown
Managing Editor: Claire Chun
Copyeditors: Elyce Petker, Abby Reser, Lauren Harrison
Front cover design: what!design @ whatweb.com
Interior design and layout: what!design @ whatweb.com

Distributed by Publishers Group West

# CONTENTS

In the Break Room 40
At the Vending Machine 41
When You're Ordering In Food 43
When You're at Lunch and the Bill Comes 44
After a Big Lunch 45
When You Send Someone on a Coffee Run 46
Before Heading into a Meeting 47
If You're Called on When Not Paying Attention in a Meeting 50
At the End of a Meeting 53
When You're Starting a Conference Call 57
When You Leave Work Early 58
At the End of the Day 60
After a Bad Day 64
When Working Late 66

**Chapter 2: Every Coworker is Unique** 69

*Meaningless Things to Say...*

To Your Personal Assistant 70
To an Intern 71
To the Building Security Guard 72
To the Person Who Hands out Office Mail 74
To the Person Who Hands out Petty Cash 75
When the Travel Coordinator Gives You Your Trip Details 76
To the Tech Support Guy When He Comes to Fix Your Computer 77
To the In-House Attorney 79
To Your Boss 80
To a Workaholic Coworker 81
To a Stressed-Out Coworker 82
To a Coworker Who Is Always on Their PDA 83
When Someone Won't Stop Talking about Their iPhone 85
To a Coworker Who Can Type Really Fast 86
When Someone Complains of Carpel Tunnel Syndrome 87
To a Coworker Who Shows Up Late for a Meeting 89

## Chapter 3: Coworkers' Personal Lives
### *Meaningless Things to Say...*

## Chapter 4: Coworkers' Hobbies and Obsessions

*Meaningless Things to Say...*

## Chapter 5: Stressful Moments at Work

*Meaningless Things to Say...*

## **Chapter 6: Office Politics**

*Meaningless Things to Say...*

## Chapter 7: Not Your Everyday Banter     231

### *Meaningless Things to Say...*

## Chapter 8: Sick Days, Holidays, Weekends and Other Days Too

*Meaningless Things to Say...*

## Chapter 9: Oh, the Places You Will Work

*Meaningless Things to Say...*

# POWER PHRASES

## MEANINGLESS ANSWERS TO COWORKERS' QUESTIONS

# INTRODUCTION

Congratulations, friend. You hold in your hands *the* foremost book on the subject of surviving social interaction in the modern office environment. With it, you are poised to take a huge step backward in genuine human contact while simultaneously taking a huge step forward in your workplace happiness, popularity, eccentricity—and possibly even career advancement.

If you don't want to become a funny-and-popular-yet-weird-and-emotionally-aloof coworker, then set this book aside to re-gift later, or perhaps you can use it to balance an extremely wobbly table. But if indeed you are looking to abandon meaningful dialogue with your coworkers and minimize the degree to which you know them and they know you—then let that table wobble.

Let's start with a small reality check: you spend huge chunks of your week with coworkers, and while most of them are fine people, they aren't all friend material. It's not that you're antisocial — it's just that you don't need to be pals with every coworker who crosses your path. Or perhaps you *are* antisocial but figure it's best to keep that between you and your therapist. Or perhaps you're just asocial. Or maybe you're somewhere in between. Maybe you don't know the difference. That's cool; neither do we.

The problem is that your coworkers have an expectation that you will develop some kind of interpersonal relationship with each of them—even though the reality of modern business is that workers are replaceable cogs who come and go as jobs get downsized, individuals transfer to other branches, and people decide to quit their job and move back into their parents' house so they can save money to start a boutique that sells high-end baby clothes.

Plus, you already have friends. You've been collecting them from the first day of kindergarten all the way through college and beyond. So even though Barry in the cubicle next to the kitchenette seems like a good guy, do you really want to spend your precious time helping him decide between a plasma or an LCD TV? One innocent word of advice in the break room on Thursday afternoon and the next thing you know, it's Saturday morning and you're helping him carry 60 inches of HDTV up four flights of stairs to his apartment. And once it's installed you gotta fire that baby up—and just like that, you're stuck watching *Days of Thunder* with your new bud and your weekend is toast.

Alas, any small talk with fellow employees is a Pandora's box that once opened, spews forth invitations to see a coworker's improv group, requests to borrow DVDs, and chronicles of allergies to dairy and wheat products. Of course, it's not like you can sit there silently and just do your actual work all day; believe us, we've tried.

It's also true that you will make some real friendships at work with some really terrific people, but this book offers a way to deal with all the other people. It provides you with entertaining, engaging and yet meaningless non-conversation starters and enders that will allow you to skate through all your daily office interactions while guaranteeing that everyone likes you and enjoys your presence. And since the categories of coworkers aren't binary, this book will come in handy with real work friends. To them you'll seem more charming, goofy and "hip to it" than ever before. To one and all, you'll seem funny and interesting. Indeed, there's no limit to how popular you will become in your office or how high you will soar.

Now go get 'em, tiger.

# HOW TO USE
# THIS BOOK

Now that you know what you need to do, how can you do it? First, understand that you will face interaction with your coworkers on many fronts. Topics ranging from their families and hobbies to corporate promotions and quarterly results are all fair game. So to make things easier, we have organized the hundreds of different situations into thematic chapters.

The first chapter covers the most common situations you will encounter at work, such as the awkward trip in the elevator or finding yourself face-to-face with a coworker in front of the coffee machine. From there, you will learn to hone your skills in all types of situations such as conversations with new interns, with the coworker who only wants to discuss sports and even some charmers for when the boss is indicted by the SEC.

Some of the sayings are easily recognizable classics that you probably have heard before while others will sound fresh and new to anyone who hears them. Either way, you have something to say that will charm, amuse, confuse and steer you out of any possible conversation.

Also sprinkled throughout the guide are meaningless answers to the most common questions that coworkers will drop on you—often without warning. These questions seem innocent, but don't let that fool you—they are nothing more than traps to suck you into a personal conversation. Once you take the bait and get inside their cubicle, be prepared for the vacation pictures to come out of the drawer.

Between each chapter is a Power Phrase. These magic bon mots can be adapted to literally any situation—never mind how they sound when they actually come out of your mouth. Always *always* keep a Power Phrase handy for moments when you get caught without a situation-specific phrase in your brain.

It's that simple. In no time at all, you'll be skilled enough to create your own meaningless phrases. If you have any questions, give us a call. If we're out of the country and you get our voicemail, just leave a message and someone will get back to you. Don't forget to include your number and the best time of day to reach you.

Thanks, and have a great day.

# POWER PHRASES

## SHOW ME THE _____.

Show me the earnings.

Show me the copier toner.

Show me the potential new hires.

Show me the birthday cake.

Show me the unauthorized time cards.

Show me the unleafted lettuce.

Show me the x-rays.

Show me the notarized documents.

Show me the PowerPoint presentation.

Show me the customer comment cards.

# CHAPTER 1
# EVERYDAY OFFICE SITUATIONS

# WHEN YOU ARRIVE AT WORK ON MONDAY MORNING

Present.

Look out world, here we come.

Is it Friday yet?

Before I do anything I just want to make sure—I'm getting paid for this, right?

Déjà vu, all over again.

Back to the grind.

Didn't the weekend just fly by?

Another day in paradise.

Fancy meeting you here.

Welcome back, fellow travelers.

On your marks...get set...WORK!

Let's kick the tires and light the fires!

Back into the ol' salt mine.

Now we get back to saving the world.

You haven't aged a bit since I last saw you on Friday afternoon.

# WHEN YOU ARRIVE AT WORK ON MONDAY MORNING

Let's be careful out there, everyone.

I like to think of us as the New Breakfast Club. I'm the jock.

Gentlemen, start your engines.

I have a good feeling about this week.

All present and accounted for?

Hope you remembered to bring your fun caps.

Here we are, just like old times.

It's nice to be back with my work family.

I wonder if there are any office birthdays this week.

Did you do the reading?

Well, onward and upward, everyone.

Another day, another dollar.

I'm really going to try to make this week special.

Let's step it up this week.

Welcome back to the Magical Mystery Tour.

# WHEN YOU ARRIVE AT WORK ON MONDAY MORNING

I had a great weekend. Just lounged around and ran a few errands.

Anyone quit over the weekend?

Who's up for some workin'?

I hope you're ready to hit this week out of the park.

I missed all of you.

Another week, another week's salary.

Let's light this candle.

Nice to be back, see you tomorrow.

This ain't no fun-day, you know?

In case you're wondering, I spent the weekend with my celebrity friends.

Push out the jive—bring in the love.

Just five more days of this and it's the weekend.

Every Monday morning is a reminder to me that I really need to check into prescription antidepressants.

Who's pumped to be here?

## "HOW ARE YOU DOING?"

Keeping on keeping on.

Just trying to keep moving forward.

Holdin' up.

Nobody knows.

Living the dream.

Just making time.

The question I ask isn't so much "how" I'm doing but rather "why" I'm doing.

Chasing the rainbow of fruit flavor.

Doing what I need to do.

Scoping the scene.

*Muy cansado. Muy, muy cansado.*

Gettin' it done.

Rockin' it.

Barely holding on.

Just working for the weekend.

I like to think that I'm keeping it real.

# TO PEOPLE WHO GET TO WORK BEFORE YOU

Sure looks like someone's bucking for a promotion.

Some people will do anything for a good parking spot.

Officer on deck!

Did your house burn down last night or something?

Don't take this the wrong way, but you're starting to make everyone else look bad.

How is that whole sleeping under your desk thing working out for you?

You're what we call in the business a "Go-Getter."

Do we get extra credit for showing up early?

Did you rent a helicopter or something?

You didn't hear this from me, but I heard they're thinking about giving you a medal.

Are you a descendent of farming folk?

You didn't look in my desk, did you? Stay out of my desk. Don't ever go in my desk.

Let me guess—you never actually went home last night.

Are you using go pills?

If only everyone arrived at work as hard as you do.

You're so early, it's already next Wednesday for you.

Looks like someone forgot to set his clocks back.

Everybody is working for the weekend—except this guy.

Oh, I forgot, it's your week to milk the company cows.

I'll see to it that you get an extra serving of rations and mead.

I wish I could show up as early as you do, but I've got my volunteer work.

Think how early you'd show up if you had a job that actually mattered.

I've been here too. I've just been making some copies.

If only the rest of them took the job as seriously as we do.

Have you ever been tested for OCD?

Did Mr. Miyagi order you to show up super early and start painting the fence?

Did you ever know that you're my hero?

Greetings, fellow environmentalists!

Oh. All of you again.

Gas money aside, I think the "us time" makes this more than worth it.

Let's stop calling it a "carpool" and start calling it a "friendpool."

You just saved the day.

Let's have a good old-fashioned sing-along today.

Shotgun!

What's Rush Limbaugh going on about today?

Oh, good. More awful music.

You ever wish your wife didn't pack your lunch in a lunch box?

Can you believe gas prices these days? It's really taking a chunk out of my vacation savings.

I feel like we hardly ever see each other anymore.

Alright. Who had the onion bagel for breakfast?

Let's ghost-ride the whip.

Whose day is it to pick the music?

I'm glad we get to do this every day.

Anyone else wanna make a run for the border?

If there's anything better than smooth jazz, I don't know what it is.

Who's ready to rock out hard?

Can we stop at Taco Bell?

I know I say this every day, but I love you guys.

If anyone touches my arm again, I'm going to lose it.

At the next stoplight—Chinese fire drill.

Can we have quiet time now?

Have you guys heard the new Radiohead album?

Can you believe those suckers sitting in traffic? I'm so glad we can take the HOV lane!

Is it cool if I smoke in here?

This car is so small that it's more like a car–hot tub than a car-pool.

My plan worked!

Wanna make a deal not to dent each other's cars today?

The only way this could be more awesome would be if we had on the same outfit.

You go in this way too?

Is that your BMW? (Point to any car in the lot.)

Race you inside.

I've got a sixer in my trunk. Want a couple of pops before we get started?

I don't know if you saw that, but the answer is, yes, I have been living in my car.

I hope someone has a pot of coffee on inside.

I like arriving around this time too.

Was parking tough?

# "HOW ARE YOU FEELING TODAY?"

I really feel like my whole life has lead up to this very moment.

Can't complain. And nobody would listen if I did.

Can I get back to you on that?

I'm still sorting that out.

I'd feel better with a drink in my hand.

Fair to middlin'.

Jazzed about life.

Never been better.

Good 'n stuff.

I get depressed a lot. Thanks for asking.

Better than that dude who got radiation-poisoned by the Russians a few years back.

I'd be feeling much better if you've got some horse tranquilizers on you.

Pretty bad. I just found out that Chairman Mao died.

I feel pretty lost right now.

Get back to me after my performance review this afternoon.

Traffic was brutal.

Big pileup on Highway 12.

Halfway here and I realize my wallet is on the dresser.

I got attacked by a bear.

Don't worry, I had Chuck clock in for me.

You guys feel the big earthquake?

I had to stop on the highway and rescue an overturned truck of puppies.

I was abducted by aliens last night and I'm still getting my bearings.

Sorry I'm late, but someone has to deliver groceries to those senior citizens.

You didn't see anything.

I had to work really late last night, and that messed up my internal clock.

I thought 9 o'clock was more of a suggestion than a rule.

Am I late? Or am I early for tomorrow? Ah-ha!

# WHEN YOU COME TO WORK HUNGOVER

Please whisper.

Anything you say can and will be used against you.

There's a freight train running through my head and the next stop is a long way off.

It's times like this when I'm really glad I didn't go into the controlled demolition business.

I heard the cure for a hangover is a Bloody Mary, but suffice it to say, that's not true.

If you need me, I'll be sleeping under my desk.

If you need to say anything to me, email it.

Seemed like a good idea at the time.

Someone please put me out of my misery.

Is there a marching band playing in the other room?

You don't want to be standing between me and the bathroom.

I just threw up in my mouth a lot.

# WHEN YOU COME TO WORK WITH A BLACK EYE

You should see the other guy's fist.

Long story.

This is what chivalry gets you these days.

Turns out resisting arrest is taken quite seriously.

At least I know I can take a punch.

I was headbutted by a dolphin, but trust me, he didn't do it on porpoise.

Did you know that when you're sitting on a bar stool, there is a bar between your face and the floor?

I'm not going to let anyone badmouth our company.

FYI, headbutting your computer doesn't restore lost spreadsheet data.

I've been training for the octagon.

# MEANINGLESS ANSWERS TO COWORKERS' QUESTIONS

## "WHAT'S NEW?"

Did you hear? They saved the world this morning.

Same old, same old.

Very little, which is how I like it.

Lots of good stuff.

My passion for pottery.

Probably a few species in Bora Bora.

Renewable energy—that's kind of a new thing, right?

The outer reaches of the universe.

Oh, I don't know...I got attacked by an alpaca on the way into work. You?

Lots of things, though none of them here.

I'm a little lonely nowadays.

Mind-bending awesomeness.

Everything in my wife's closet.

Everything in my husband's golf bag.

# TO A COWORKER WITH WHOM YOU SHARE AN OFFICE

Home sweet home.

So where are you from? [Note: Ask every day.]

I see you more than I see my own family.

Let's pimp this place out.

Two men enter...one man leaves.

How would you feel about making this a strictly "no-shirt" office?

Just so you know, my favorite color is rust.

We should get some disaster supplies for this place, just in case.

Just an FYI, I'm what we call a "Day-Snorer."

Do you think we should permit smoking?

Just so you know, there's a place in my head where I go to hide.

I've decided to start calling this place The Dragon's Lair.

I think we should get a few plants to add some color. There are some species that do really great with indoor light.

Would it be cool if I put up my Faith Hill poster?

# TO A COWORKER WITH WHOM YOU SHARE AN OFFICE

What do you say we replace our printer with a kegerator?

What this place needs is an Ikea run.

Do you want to switch desks, just for today?

I already talk like you but when I start looking like you, it's over!

I don't want to make a big thing out of this, but did you take a Post-It?

I like sharing an office with you, but I think there's only enough oxygen for one.

Do you think we could beat the other cubicles in a fight?

We need to a figure out an office flatulence policy.

I know it's six times more likely to kill us than an intruder, but how would you feel about getting a gun?

Whose turn is it to call in the bomb threat?

Is there a loud screaming noise coming from directly below us?

Welcome to the Biodome.

This is where the magic happens.

Hi, neighbors.

I call mine my "cubie," which is short for "cubicle."

Can you close the door of your cubicle? You're talking kind of loud.

I don't mind the lack of doors, but I could really go for a ceiling so I can put my boy band posters up there.

I like that we all kind of have our own area but they're all connected at the same time.

Interesting tidbit—the first cubicle was invented by Leonardo da Vinci.

I love what you've done with the place.

It's really cozy in here.

You should install a fireplace.

I like how it has a built-in skylight.

If you knocked down a couple of these walls, it would really open this place up.

Maybe we should form a neighborhood crime watch.

This cubicle is not big enough for the two of us. And I don't mean that in an angry way.

This is where I go to hide.

The thing I like about cubicles is that they just feel classy.

I like to stand on a chair and look over at my neighbors until they notice that I'm staring at them.

A man's cube is his pathetic castle.

Have you thought about throwing down some hardwood floors in here?

So…give me the tour.

Someday I hope to have a whole cube.

I love the feeling of the wind in my hair provided by an open-air cubicle.

I couldn't help but overhear everything.

# MEANINGLESS ANSWERS TO COWORKERS' QUESTIONS

## "WHERE ARE YOU OFF TO?"

To find my destiny.

Big dance party downtown.

To fight crime.

Volunteering.

My laundry is taunting me.

Gotta get my hair washed.

Gotta get drunk.

I'm on the lam.

My Fortress of Solitude.

Ninja classes.

There's a panther loose in my apartment and I gotta figure a way to coax him outta there.

There's an all-comers slam-poetry contest that I gotta emcee.

I work the night shift at the morgue.

Gonna burn it down like a couple of clowns.

Daddy needs his juice.

It ain't great, but the price is right.

Time to feed the ulcer.

Coffee is more important than knowledge.

Gotta get some gas in my tank. I'm running on fumes.

The coffee's really hot today.

That's the smell I like to hear.

I'll be honest...I don't trust anyone who doesn't drink coffee.

Would it kill them to put in a latte machine?

Pulling into the docking station for refueling.

Is it just me, or does this coffee have a hint of coriander?

The way I see it, they can keep their dental and vision plan so long as the free coffee keeps on flowing.

Ah...beachwood aged.

I've had better coffee at the tire store.

# AT THE
# COFFEE MACHINE

My grandfather used to say you could tell a lot about a man by how much coffee he drank. Of course, he also thought he could tell if someone was a vampire by how much blood they drank, so...you know...grain of salt.

I'm not sure what I love more, the flavor or the caffeine. Just kidding, it's the caffeine.

What was that waiter's name again? Oh—that's right—Jean Luc.

Is it possible this is decaf? I've already had seven cups and I don't feel a thing.

Don't freak out—but I've only had half a cup of this stuff and I already can't feel my face.

I've been trying to get them to replace this thing with a kegerator for years.

Have you ever heard the theory that coffee was responsible for the Enlightenment?

Is this instant?

Where's that hot precious Joe?

Can't we just do away with the decaf pot and use that burner for more of the regular coffee that productive employees drink?

# AT THE COFFEE MACHINE

Caffeine is a gateway drug to good times!

How about some social networking 1.0-style?

They gotta make these pots bigger—am I right?

I read once that coffee is the key to a happy life. Granted, it was in a pamphlet from the Coffee Council, but it still made a lot of sense.

I'm having a paradigm shift from regular to decaf.

I call this the coffee widget.

I'm so hyped-up on coffee I can't even see straight.

Do you want to trade cups?

Coffee breath is not talked about enough.

Juan Valdez truly is my American hero.

Coffee is this generation's smoke break.

Coffee snobs are worse than wine snobs. Just give me the mud and send me on my way.

Ah, my dear friend Coffee. You're the only one who truly understands me.

## MEANINGLESS ANSWERS TO COWORKERS' QUESTIONS

## "WILL YOU TAKE A LOOK AT SOMETHING FOR ME?"

They have doctors now, you know.

I'm happy to, but whatever you need to ask me is probably on the Internet.

Is it a surprise party for me? Because if it is, then YES I CAN!

Is it a bag of money from a drug deal gone bad that you came across while hunting on the Texas prairie? Because then I want nothing to do with it.

Is it pure, uncut cocaine? Because if it is, then YES I WILL!

You didn't accidentally hit a pedestrian on the way to work today, did you?

I suppose it'd be super weird if I said no, so, sure.

It's nothing illegal, is it?

I'll look but I won't touch.

Let me guess—it's a can of peanuts with a lid you can't open. I wasn't born yesterday.

Where's the eject button?

Does this thing make waffles?

How in the name of Oprah does this thing work?

You sit on it, I'll stand guard.

Do you ever push all the buttons at once so everyone has to stop at every floor?

Ever wonder how we put a man on the moon but we can't make a copier that works for more than two consecutive days at a time?

Did you know that the guys who work on these things make like half a million dollars a year?

Watch your sleeves around that intake area. At my last gig a guy got his arm ripped clean off.

How many years until this thing takes all our jobs?

I bet if Johannes Gutenberg had known his work would eventually lead to this, he would have kept his fancy ideas to himself.

I heard that in Japan they have a copier the size of a stick of gum.

Mark my words, someday they will come out with a copier that does color.

Apparently Elvis had seventeen copiers in Graceland and would sit on his couch and watch them making copies all at once.

Remember when cell phones were this big?

It's sad how all the small mom 'n' pop copier makers got gobbled up by the big copier conglomerates.

Initiate self-destruct sequence.

Well, copier, I see we meet again.

How did they ever do this job without this thing?

Do you call it a "copier" or a "copy machine"?

Here we are, living out our childhood dreams.

Are you ticklish?

Have you tried the cyan toner? De-licious.

Sorry, did I leave my porn in there?

Is this the line for the bathroom?

Slow down. Paper doesn't grow on trees, you know.

I'm having a total déjà vu right now. I could have sworn I saw that document before.

If any paper jams go down, I got your back.

How about they make the toner cartridge bigger? How about that for innovation?

If we break it now, we can go home early.

If I make a copy of my face will I get a tan?

This copier loves me. I can feel it.

I like warming my hands on the glass. It's toasty.

Maybe it would work if I brought it an offering of carbon paper as a sacrifice.

Since we're on the fifteenth floor anyway, why don't we see if this thing can fly?

# WHEN PASSING SOMEONE IN THE HALL

There she is!

Working hard or hardly working?

I wouldn't go that way if I were you.

Lookin' good.

Here comes trouble!

Give me a fist-bump.

Keep doing what you're doing.

Looking sharp!

Like two ships passing in the hallway.

We should do this more often.

For real.

Keep on truckin'!

How are ya. [Note: not a question]

Handsomer by the minute.

Looking right, doing good.

I know this guy is up to no good!

# WHEN PASSING
# SOMEONE IN THE HALL

Look at that powerwalking!

Whatever you're doing, it's working.

I can't help but notice your powerful gait.

Now starting as quarterback for the New York Giants, number 16 (*coworker's name*)!

I'd probably turn around now if I were you.

In case you're wondering, I'm sneaking out to buy gum.

Here you come...and there you go.

Ramming speed!

Careful if you're going that way—there's a puma on the loose.

Does the ceiling seem lower today?

You just disproved the old adage that you can't walk and be awesome at the same time.

Don't worry, this will be over soon.

I love those pants.

Happy hunting.

# WHEN PASSING SOMEONE IN THE HALL

Hold your head up.

Fancy meeting you like this.

I'm just trying to work off lunch, how about you?

Let's walk really fast and look very busy.

Wanna try for the Doppler Effect?

Turn around while you still can.

VEER RIGHT, VEER RIGHT!

Into the great beyond.

Did you ping me?

Don't look at me! I'm hideous!

The boss is looking for you. Kidding.

You been losing weight?

You da man.

I can't believe you still work here.

Free donuts in accounting.

Be careful of turf toe.

We have liftoff.

Welcome to the world's most disappointing theme park ride.

Thanks for not making me do this on my own.

I'm glad we finally got some "us time."

Let's never speak of this moment. Ever.

I wonder what kind of bandwidth this thing gets.

Ever wonder how these things work?

This device is where the term "elevator music" comes from.

Why don't they have elevators that go side-to-side so you don't have to walk down the hall to get an ice cream sandwich?

I usually take the stairs, but I'm wearing the wrong shoes.

Let's take this thing all the way to the top of the food chain.

Where's Willie Wonka when he need him?

If we get stuck in here, I want you to promise to eat me first.

Did you know that a colloquial Arabic word for elevator, "*ahsahnseer*," comes from the French word for elevator, "*ascenseur*"?

# IN THE ELEVATOR

I used to always take the stairs. Then I blew out my ACL.

Fun fact: the Greeks and Romans had elevators. Really inefficient, terribly unsafe elevators.

Would it kill them to install just one escalator?

I know I'm going to three and you're going to four, but if you want to stop at four first, I totally understand.

For what it's worth, if I had to get stuck in an elevator for several hours with anyone, it'd be you.

When do you think elevators will get those pneumatic doors like on Star Trek?

I wish we had an elevator operator to push the buttons. We could call him Bits or Henry and tip him during the holiday season. And whenever we got on the elevator he'd ask us how the markets are.

Imagine if we brought a tribesman from the Amazon on this thing. He'd flip out.

Whoa...is this moving?

Do you think if you take a dog on an elevator, they know they're going up and down? Or do you think they just think the doors close, they stand there for a minute, and then the doors open and the whole world has changed?

Someone in here earlier went nuts with the cologne.

I'll stay on this side. You stay on that side.

Weeeeeeeeeeeeeeeeeeee!

Does that close button even work?

Where do I stick the quarters?

This is bigger than my apartment.

Have you ever ridden on top of this thing?

I'd take the stairs, but I am lazy and a bit of an underachiever.

If we go more than five floors together, are we dating?

The next person who walks on, I'm gonna punch.

Somebody has stolen thirteen.

One for the money, two for the show, three to get ready now go vator go!

I'm going only one floor. Please don't judge me.

# "CAN YOU LOOK AT SOMETHING ON MY COMPUTER?"

Oh, you don't want my help.

Things can't be going well if you're comin' to me.

OK, but it will surely make me more full of myself.

If it's Star Trek fan fiction, you've come to the right place.

Do I have to talk after I look at it?

Only if I can get half your sandwich at lunch.

Not now. I'm buying a lot of Beanie Babies on eBay.

You know I'm incapable of offering objective advice, right?

Is there an Old Navy gift card in it for me?

Can I have your salary for the time I'm looking at it and you're just sitting there?

Looking is my specialty.

OK, but I won't promise you I'll be happy about it.

You have no idea how long I've been waiting for you to ask me that.

We gotta stop meeting like this.

Are you following me?

Quick heads up—I have a wide stance.

Things just got really, really, really, really, really weird.

I know everyone says this, but lets really try to keep in touch this summer.

If I could whistle, I'd be whistling right now. You know, to make things less awkward.

It's this sort of thing that makes me wish I could just hold it until I got home.

You bring beer?

Who's got the smokes?

Would you mind looking at a mole for me?

Someday I'm gonna go into the bathroom, shave my head, come out and never mention a word of it to anyone. And if anyone asks what happened to my hair, I'm gonna say, "It was like this this morning."

I'm just decluttering my bladder.

Don't get any ideas if you see me tapping my foot in the stall next to you—I've had that Fergalicious song stuck in my head all week.

Would anyone notice if we just hid out in here all day?

We should just start having our meetings in here.

Live the dream.

I read somewhere that the typical workplace bathroom has over seven trillion bacteria. Just a little FYI.

And so, we find ourselves in the great equalizer of squalor.

That's Larry Craig's favorite stall. Not the senator, the guy in shipping.

This reminds me of the last time we used the bathroom together.

You see the numbers from the Mitchell account? I haven't and I don't know what that is, but I thought saying that would make this seem more casual.

Does this look infected?

I always find this to be way, way, way, way more uncomfortable than it needs to be, and talking about it just makes it worse.

# IN THE BATHROOM

This place is giving me a lot of great ideas for the master bath I'm fixing up at home.

The black crow sleeps at night in the old barn.

Funny story but true: in high school I was voted most likely to go to the bathroom with a stranger.

I'll hide first and you count to fifty.

Can I get a woop woop?

In case there's a problem in there, do we have all your current emergency contact info?

I hear they're going to take the doors off all the stalls to cut down on office-supply theft.

Gotta get my eight glasses.

I taste a hint of oak.

The ol' watering hole.

Since we're both here, I guess we should gossip.

Do you hate Bill in shipping as much as I do?

How much of a cliché are we right now?

The secrets this cooler would tell if it could talk.

Would it kill them to put Kool-Aid in this thing?

I really need to start bringing in my own glass.

Did you know that the human body is 98 percent water? The rest is other things.

It sure is nice of them to give us all this free water. Someone upstairs must really care.

I hear you cop a pretty nice buzz if you drink a couple gallons of this stuff.

Now that we're all properly hydrated, let's get back to work.

I miss the hormones in tap water.

# AT THE DRINKING FOUNTAIN

Gotta get my eight glasses.

Nothing refreshes like a quick drink of lukewarm water.

Tell you what I could use—a coffee fountain.

Do you think the company is required by law to provide a drinking fountain?

In the event of a chemical spill, this could easily double as an eyewash fountain.

I call it the "two-hydrogens-and-one-oxygen" fountain.

I forgot to brush this morning and I need my flouride.

Do you think they have drinking fountains in prison?

Why don't they have these outside more? That'd be nice.

Let's agree to the five-second rule.

Moment on the lips, a lifetime on the hips.

This is so much more eco-friendly than everyone drinking bottled water all day.

I hope they recycle the water that doesn't make it into your mouth.

# IN THE BREAK ROOM

What are you doing here?

Shouldn't you be working?

Fancy meeting you here.

OK, good. We're all here now.

How did you get a reservation for this place?

What's today's special?

Wanna go through the couch cushions and look for change?

We need a ping pong table in here.

Can we put on *Oprah*?

You're sitting at my table.

I'll make more coffee.

Is it that hard to install a few hammocks?

Are you planning to stay in here for your whole entire break?

I prefer to think of this as the "breakdown room."

Some granite countertops and hardwood floors would really spruce this place up.

What's good?

I'm just going to push all the buttons at once and whatever I get, I get.

You hold one side, I'll take the other, and we're gonna shake this till I get a Kit Kat.

Does this thing have Prozac?

There goes the diet.

Oprah and Dr. Oz say that this is just going to spike my blood sugar.

This is my favorite place in the entire office.

Moment on the lips, a lifetime in my arteries.

So many options, so little time.

Are Cheetos a chip?

This thing is my only friend in this place.

Oh dear, I sure hope that it's true that chocolate improves your mood.

Whatever became of those pills on *The Jetsons*? Add some water and boom, you get a steak dinner.

# MEANINGLESS ANSWERS TO COWORKERS' QUESTIONS

## "WANT TO GO TO LUNCH?"

Together?

Only if you let me pay in nickels.

I'm fasting till we get a handle on global warming.

I'm on a special diet. I'm only eating alone right now.

You don't want to see me eating. It's very unpleasant.

I'm meeting my college roommate today actually.

I gotta spend my lunch hour doing my receipts.

I'm scared of lunches.

You know I chew with my mouth open and drink through my nose, right?

I brought a bag of oats from home.

Would we be sitting at the same table?

Yeah. I can always use an extra set of hands when I go dumpster diving.

I usually work out during my lunch hour.

If you're trying to ask me out, say so now.

When are you going—around lunchtime?

# WHEN YOU'RE ORDERING IN FOOD

What's your price point for lunch?

We're outsourcing lunch today.

At the rate we get things done, we'll have lunch here sometime tomorrow.

I love ordering lunch. It's like a picnic at work!

When the food comes, let's all grab at the bags at once.

Just like momma used to make.

This is smart because the money we spend on food we more than make up for by time saved having to cook here in the office.

Let's get ethnic food so we can all feel sophisticated.

# WHEN YOU'RE AT LUNCH AND THE BILL COMES

Now the other shoe drops.

This is gonna hurt.

If you'll excuse me, I have to go to the bathroom and climb out the window.

OK...who here knows how to fake food poisoning?

Well, I'm expected back at the office, so I should probably be going....

Let's figure out which of us makes the most money and do it that way.

Do you think they take pesos?

Let's all guess at the amount of the bill and whoever is farthest away has to pay.

Maybe they'll let us pay for our meal by washing dishes.

Unfortunately, all my credit cards have been repossessed by the bank.

Oh dear, I really don't like this part.

Think we can get reimbursed in petty cash?

Time for some credit card roulette.

Stick a fork in me, because I am done.

I feel a food coma coming on.

This is why we need nap time at work.

I have no idea how I'm gonna get through four more hours of work.

And to think I ate three breakfasts this morning.

I could really use a digestif.

This is going straight to my hips.

Anyone want a cappuccino?

Now who's up for some tacos?

I should join a gym.

I gotta start going to the gym I pay thirty dollars a month to belong to.

I could really use a piece of pie, a toothpick and some of those diet pills that put holes in your heart.

That's it—I'm getting my stomach stapled.

# WHEN YOU SEND SOMEONE ON A COFFEE RUN

We're going out-of-house for coffee.

Don't forget the creamer!

I think this fits right into your wheelhouse.

Today, you are our hero.

We run on coffee runs.

I take mine caffeinated.

There's a bonus in it for you if you get back here in ten minutes or less.

You fly, I buy...for myself. You're still on your own.

Find Joe and bring him to me.

I drink only Yuban.

Make sure it's hot!

See if they have one of those carrying trays for the cups. We can use it to build a hat.

This is the most important part of any day.

# BEFORE HEADING INTO A MEETING

Time to stand and deliver.

Is there going to be a test on this later?

Might want to make a quick pit stop before takeoff.

Gentlemen, start your engines.

Do I look fat in this?

Do it to it.

Reporting for duty.

Did you bring your oxygen tanks?

Bad news, guys. Bill Gates won't be coming after all.

See you on the other side.

Give 'em hell, Harry.

Let's all try to remember Rule #1: Have fun.

Do you think we'll need our staplers?

I'll distract them and you make a break for it.

I can feel a paradigm shift coming.

Let's be careful out there, gentlemen.

People always say, "Work hard, play hard." Well, I like to think this is both.

This is why we, or at least some people in this company, make the big bucks.

It's game time, baby!

Smoke 'em if you got 'em.

This is going to hurt.

I hope we don't humiliate ourselves. That's all I can hope for, really.

Maybe I'll use this meeting as an opportunity to come out of the closet.

This is where we separate the men from the boys.

If we start driving now, we can be in Mexico by sundown.

I hope this wraps up soon. I've got to get home and punch myself in the face.

Boy oh boy, do I ever hope we get more memos.

Do you have your cyanide pill ready?

Let's give 'em the old dog and pony show.

# BEFORE HEADING INTO A MEETING

I wonder if we're gonna finally find out the mystery of the island.

When are we finally gonna get to dissect a cat?

Do you think the CEO will be there?

I live for this stuff.

I'm usually really nervous for these things, but today I feel really calm.

Please have bagels inside, please have bagels inside, please have bagels inside.

I brought a pillow, you know, just in case.

Is this BYOB?

If we are supposed to be thinking outside the box, can I stay out here?

I doubt anyone in there knows my name.

Place this cardboard cutout of me in my seat and they won't notice.

I hope I get eliminated first.

Can I cheat off of you?

I can't comment without giving this more consideration.

You've left me speechless.

Yahtzee!

I can really see the advantages of all options.

Before I comment, let's take a vote.

Don't ask me, let's run it by marketing.

No comment.

Can I buy a vowel?

I say we GO for it.

Sorry, I was thinking about *Oprah*.

I'm going to need to see more data.

You don't want to know what I'm thinking right now.

That's not in my wheelhouse.

Ooof. Lot to digest there.

Ping me later after I have time to think about this.

I'm going to need my Magic Eight Ball for this one.

I make such little money here, I can't afford to pay attention. Get it?

I need a moment because I have to choose my words wisely.

I'm gonna pass, Bob.

I'm sorry, I've been obsessing over that amazing shirt you're wearing.

Give me that in laymen's terms.

Well...I'm torn...what's everyone else think?

Lots to work off there.

I might need to read it a few times in writing to really process all that.

I'd like to assert my Fifth Amendment rights.

## MEANINGLESS ANSWERS TO COWORKERS' QUESTIONS

### "HOW'S IT GOING?"

Slowly but painfully.

Down the line.

Damning the torpedoes.

I think I lost my tambourine.

I'm a little lonely these days.

I'm so hungry, I'm about to fall over.

My senses have been stripped.

I wish I knew.

North by northwest.

I'll leave that judgment to historians.

Straight into the gutter.

My new nickname is 24601.

I'm too close to things to know.

I've been better, I've been worse, and also who cares?

Like a bear after honey.

Better than I ever thought possible.

Now...who's ready to take the quiz?

Can I go home now?

Seacrest...out!

Please submit all questions in writing to human resources.

I've done all I can do here, now it's up to you.

With that, it's martini time.

Everyone feel good?

It's go time.

Anyone else tired?

OK, now it's on to bigger and better things.

If you take anything away from this meeting, it should be a pencil and anything else you brought in with you.

So in summation, you just got "punk'd."

When you leave this room, consider this the first day of the rest of your life.

Now don't screw this up.

# AT THE END OF A MEETING

Anyway, it must be happy hour somewhere. Let's roll.

If you're still confused about the project at this point, don't tell anyone.

Remember: you don't have any excuses after this.

We're all cool here, right?

And, on a personal note, it's great to be here with my best friends in the whole entire world.

Thanks for having me. Doing a presentation for you guys was one of my New Year's resolutions.

Do you guys validate?

Remember: the journey of a thousand miles begins with a single step.

You didn't buy any of that did you? I was just making it up as I went along.

Let's hurry up and finish so we can all give each other back rubs.

I hope you all learned something and had a little fun along the way.

Look out world, here we come.

This project will be our Waterloo. But in a good way.

That was a good one.

I'm a better person than I was when I walked in.

If Tony Robbins could have been here for this meeting, he would have been proud.

I think we made some good progress, but more importantly, we got to know each other a little better.

That's a lot to think about. Let's all digest that and meet back here tomorrow.

Marinate on that for a while.

Peace, I'm outta here!

So let's just consider today as "Day Zero."

So, I think we figured that out. Now—on to world peace.

I don't think of this as a meeting—I think of it as a "funning."

Who's up for another one?

That was illuminating.

Lots of good stuff came out of this, I think.

Let's do it again soon.

What's your plan for how to end the meeting?

Lot of upside happening in here. I can feel it.

Can't wait for the next one.

And they said that wasn't going to be horrible.

I wasn't even supposed to be here.

Anyone else got a wicked leg cramp?

Does this mean I have to go back to work now?

OK, let's wango tango.

Is it unrealistic of me to think that we will all be doing this again soon?

My subordinate will call your subordinate.

How about a play date?

Steady as she goes, gentlemen.

Well, nothing accomplished again.

Open a line of communication, Lieutenant Uhuru.

Let's make an effort to not all talk at the same time and to respect boundaries.

Who's got the conch?

You can't see it, but I'm not wearing any pants.

Nobody freak out—this is just like a normal phone call, only with more people.

Wanna start off with some small talk?

I say we kick things off by each saying one nice thing about the other people on the call.

If anyone hears clicking, it's because we're being investigated by the FBI for fraud and they've tapped out phones.

It's good to hear everyone's voices again.

Even though we're on the phone, I still feel like I'm right there with everyone.

Good night, you princes of Maine, you kings of New England.

Please don't hate me for getting out early.

This is when all my sucking up really pays dividends.

I guess the parole board bought my story.

So long, suckers.

Well, you guys might want to learn to fake sick too.

Freeeee-dom!!!!

I hope I make it to the perimeter before the guards notice.

I think I've figured out an escape plan.

I'm thinking about leaving my jacket on my chair so the bosses think I'm still here. I've heard they do that in France.

The company's loss is TGI Friday's gain.

I'm sorry to tell you this, but I'm going home now.

I guess I just work much more quickly than the rest of you.

## MEANINGLESS ANSWERS TO COWORKERS' QUESTIONS

## "DID YOU GET THE MEMO?"

About the new policy regarding sneezing in the office?

No! I better get back to my office! Stat!

I stopped reading the memos years ago.

If I did, it's a distant memo-ry by now.

I probably did get it, but then just threw it out before I looked at it.

About the killer bees?

Did it say there were leftover muffins in the kitchen? Because then I wish I had read it.

I figured I'd wait for the movie.

Was it an e-memo? I'm totally electronic now.

Was it sent through my assistant?

Nope. Back to you in the studio, Ted.

If it wasn't on ESPN, I didn't see it.

I'm going to finish reading the last *Harry Potter* book first.

No. Don't tell me how it ends!

Another day, another dollar.

Good night you princes of Maine, you kings of New England.

My work here is done.

Everyone remember to Wang Chung tonight.

I guess the real problems of the world will have to wait another day.

Tonight, I will sleep the sleep of the just.

Before you take off, can you do me a favor? Have a really great night.

Don't worry, we'll always be together in our hearts.

That was fun. How about we do it again tomorrow, say 9 a.m.?

I just want you guys to know that I've never worked with such an incredible and professional group of people. In fact, I consider you my best friends in the whole world.

Hey, do you guys take your ties off at night?

Remember to eat dinner.

Someone bring a camera tomorrow.

Do you guys think I'm OK to drive?

Everyone loaded up on office supplies? OK, let's get out of here.

Let's make like Macaulay Culkin and go home alone.

Let's just hope that for one more night our wives haven't run off with the guy from the gym.

If you need me, I'll be at home, staring at the walls, crying a little.

Sleepy now. Me go home.

I hate goodbyes, so I'll just say hello for tomorrow now. Hello.

Don't look back. Just go. Just go.

Let's all go home to contemplate what we accomplished today.

Today we finished the Shafer account. Tomorrow, we take down cancer—who's with me?

Are you gonna be at the 6:15 a.m. Pilates class tomorrow?

Hey, if you're gonna party tonight, party hard—but party safe.

Hey, wear a seatbelt. Accounts receivable needs you healthy.

If we don't survive the night, it was an honor knowing you.

Nothing is more satisfying than a hard day's honest work, and if I ever find out what that's like, I'll call you.

Remind me: why do we do this again?

I think we added value today.

Anyone wanna race to the parking lot?

Tomorrow is yet another day to work hard and get nothing done.

Let's act like today never happened.

Be careful out there.

Now I gotta change into my costume and go fight crime.

Let's get drunk and not come into work tomorrow.

Did the sun even come out today?

I need a drink to wash away my tears.

It feels so good to be so done.

Now it's time for me to change into a bat.

Now's the part where I stop caring.

I've gotta get home and work on my scrapbook.

If we get outta here now, we may see our kids before they graduate.

Time to go get home to my wife. Now the work really starts.

Try to take some quiet time tonight to just appreciate the little things.

Happy hunting.

Sweet. We don't even have to come back until tomorrow.

Call my cell if there's an emergency—it's already turned off.

You guys. We did it. We finally did it.

Remember to have a vegetable tonight.

I think there's some stuff on TV tonight if you get bored.

Enjoy your freedom. Try to decompress.

One day closer to the weekend.

At the end of the day, it's the end of day.

# AFTER A BAD DAY

Well, we've had the devil's own day, haven't we?

Lick 'em tomorrow, though.

No point in giving up now.

Just gotta keep moving.

It's all gonna be all right.

Put this day behind you.

Let's just shepherd in the good times, starting tomorrow.

I feel like we should light some sage.

# "WHAT DO YOU THINK THIS MEETING IS ABOUT?"

Probably something about you not cleaning up after yourself in the office kitchen.

Maybe we're all getting big bonuses. No, actually I have no idea.

Peace, love and harmony?

Probably just to tell us what a great job we all do.

Maybe we're all just gonna have a good sit.

Maybe it's one of those dinner theater mystery deals. That'd be fun.

Maybe they brought in a petting zoo for the day.

It's an intervention. For you.

I don't think it's anyone's business what it's about.

If I had to guess, I'd say it's a firearms safety course.

Maybe they want everyone to sexually harass each other so we can get it out of our systems.

I don't know, but you think it's cool if I take off my shoes?

I bet they hired a magician to entertain us.

# WHEN WORKING LATE

And the winner is...not me.

If I were unemployed, I'd be home right now.

Forget places that deliver dinner, we need a place that delivers breakfast.

Let's try to think of this as a sleepover party.

Who brought the pep pills?

Anyone mind if I crash out for a few hours under the conference table?

I didn't want to see my beloved family tonight anyway.

How fortunate that we're all married to our jobs and not to real people, huh?

I'll be back in a minute. I'm going to take off my pants and sit in the boss' chair.

Can we expense dinner? What about uppers?

Once the sun sets, I start to itch.

Anyone want to use my nose hair clipper?

This is seriously going to cut into my drinking time.

Can we at least use the email to tell our families where we are?

Enough of this burning the midnight oil. Hasn't anyone heard of global warming?

I'm just going to run home, grab a bite to eat, watch *CSI*, shower, sleep for eight hours and then I'll come back.

Don't think of it as working late today. Think of it as starting tomorrow really early.

This has a very *Lord of the Flies* feel to it.

Guess I'm not gonna make the block party this year.

We're getting paid extra for this, right?

If we were vampires, this would just be called "working."

They gotta put a shower in this place. Then we could just live here.

Anyone here know anything about the art of arson?

Meet me on the roof in fifteen; we're going to howl at the moon.

I always feel weird being in the office after hours. It's like I'm breaking in or something.

Work harder, not smarter. That's what I always say.

# POWER PHRASES

## YOU REALLY PUT THE _____ IN _____.

You really put the random in randomization strategy.

You really put the man in manicure.

You really put the physical in physical therapy.

You really put the anal in cost analysis.

You really put the engine in engineer.

You really put the sold in soldering.

You really put the style in hairstylist.

You really put the copy in copywriting.

You really put the real in realtor.

You really put the me in mechanic.

# CHAPTER 2
# EVERY COWORKER
# IS UNIQUE

One more time…what's your name again?

You remember to get me those tickets for Turandot? Just kidding. I hate culture.

Just because I'm your boss we can't be friends.

Can you call Bono's personal assistant and see if he wants to do lunch?

I was told that you're not to do "my" personal errands anymore, so today I'd like to pick up my wife's dry-cleaning.

Drop and give me twenty. Just kidding. Make it ten.

Could you please do a better job of averting your eyes when I come in?

I'm like Santa, and you're my little elf.

For this to work, you have to promise you're not going to ever make a mistake.

Just know that I know what's going on when I'm not looking.

Please schedule some time for us to get to know each other in the next six months.

You make me a better person.

One more time...what's your name again?

Lisa, right? No, that was the last intern. Don't tell me. I know this one. Ron?

Welcome to the magic.

If you pay close enough attention, you will learn how to do everything. Not really though.

I was young like you once. Then this job stole my youth.

When is that new Linkin Park album dropping?

If you ever need some advice, please text me. Or IM. Whatevs.

Don't trust anyone over thirty. Except me.

Listen to me very carefully: get out while you can. They're going to harvest your organs.

I hear the draft is coming back.

Here's some advice for you: better to remain silent and be thought a fool than to open your mouth and remove all doubt.

If you think you're going to replace me, you're sorely mistaken. Wait...actually you might be right.

Wazzzzzup!

What's new?

Is the area secure?

Anyone try to sneak in today?

We should set up a perimeter.

Do you want to bother with the whole names thing or are you cool?

The all-seeing eye of Saruman.

Anything good on the TV monitors?

That digital TV conversion must have hit you and your security guard brotherhood pretty hard, huh?

I've been working with my boss on getting you a gun.

Keepin' busy?

Watcha watchin'?

Is that *American Idol*?

All quiet on the Western Front?

# "CAN I ASK YOU A QUESTION?"

Anything. Wait. On second thought, no.

It's against company policy. Memo came out yesterday.

Nothing would make me happier.

I handled one question already today. That's my limit.

The answer is yes. I do work out.

Yes, but you shouldn't question authority.

Is it one of those weird questions that's really just veiled criticism that's going to make me hate you a lot?

If the question is how I keep my hair this shiny and full of bounce, yes.

Is it a rhetorical one?

I'd love to see you try.

I don't hug.

Do you think you'd be better off looking within yourself for the answer?

I'm not sure if I'm ready to get hurt again.

# TO THE PERSON WHO HANDS OUT OFFICE MAIL

Mail call!

Let me guess—nothing but bills, right?

Any care packages? I could go for some chocolate and cigarettes right now.

Neither rain nor sleet or snow nor free donuts in the downstairs kitchen can keep you from delivering the invitations to trade shows.

There's no shame in starting in the mail room. You should ask the CEO about her days in the mail room.

Do you need this back?

So...same time tomorrow?

Delivering the mail showcases your organizational skills, efficiency and mail-delivery skills.

Apparently George Washington got his start by delivering the mail in the White House.

Did you check this for anthrax?

Any paper cuts today?

# TO THE PERSON WHO HANDS OUT PETTY CASH

Here comes my favorite person.

Uh-oh, I hope this isn't a random receipt check.

Did you properly adjust the *per diem* for inflation and my drinking habits?

Where's all your money?

I hope someone is watching the money while you're away.

What's the company's guns 'n dope allowance these days?

You should travel with a security team.

Just in time. I need to get some cash to my bookie by lunch or he is going to break my thumbs.

I hope you're looking for me!

Hey, it's one of those new walking ATMs.

Come on now, daddy needs a new pair of shoes.

Actually, if you have them, my supplier prefers to get paid in rupees.

Just keep going—I'll say "when" after I have enough.

Looks like happy hour is going to be extra happy tonight.

It's go time.

I hope the hotel offers a continental breakfast.

Thank you, Miss Moneypenny.

I'm going to need an alias in case the heat gets on me.

I'd like my petty cash in Krugerrands.

If you need to get a hold of me, I'll be checking into the hotel under the name Vanna White.

As we say in the biz—let's get this show on the road.

This tape will self destruct in 10 seconds.

You did get me the Presidential suite, correct?

I am to mini bars what Yogi Bear is to picnic baskets.

If I don't make it back, please tell my family I loved them.

What's our emergency exit strategy?

Who's my handler?

Who booked this? You know I only fly first class.

Oh, hi. Sorry. I don't recognize you when you're not seated at my desk.

Let's hope no one's computer is crashing right now.

Can you install Donkey Kong for me?

It stopped working after I put a piece of baloney in the disk drive. Not going to do that again.

Do you even have a desk or do you just wait for one of us to call you?

Before you go, remind me to show you this video of a monkey sniffing his own butt.

Is Excel the one where you locate and destroy the mines?

Have you ever looked for answers on this Google? It's amazing.

I already kicked it and threw water on it, so I'm really open to any and all ideas right now.

So, who's got the most porn on their computer?

I got some emails with really cool attachments I'm gonna forward to you. Cool?

Before you sit down—what's the password?

# "CAN I ASK YOU
A PERSONAL QUESTION?"

Not without my attorney present.

With me, there is no personal.

Nothing would make me happier or more
uncomfortable.

Hooray!

And why wouldn't you?

Please. Perhaps you can learn from my mistakes.

Only if I can ask you one in return.

About me or somebody else? Because that's
important.

Yes. Now ask the second one.

Is it about me?

33.

Sure, but let's step into my panic room first.

What if I say no?

Sure. Let's make things even more awkward.

Yes. And the answer is the yoga.

Sue anyone today?

How goes the law?

I slipped and fell in the bathroom today and my neck is killing me. Do you have time to talk to me now?

Ah, the law...those wise constraints that make men free.

Ever clerk?

I would imagine that being in-house counsel is much more rewarding on a day-to-day basis than working at a big corporate law firm.

Do lawyers ever get really drunk and jokingly call it "passing the bar"?

Hey there, Perry Mason.

Hey there, Ironsides.

Hey there, Atticus Finch.

Can I get your advice? I may have accidentally killed my next door neighbor.

Are you wearing your legal briefs?

I'll see you in court.

Hi, boss. (Keep walking.)

Did you do something with your hair? It looks really good.

(Distracted) Oh, hey there. Sorry, I can't stop thinking about the Henderson account.

You remind me of my father.

I bet you do really well with the ladies.

You and I would have been best buddies in high school.

*Hola, jefe.*

There's our general!

Here's our hero!

You're a real man of the people.

Looking good, champ.

Have you been working out?

What was the most important lesson of your working life?

Careful you don't cut someone! Because that suit is sharp.

You've really inspired me.

Do you even have a home?

You love you some work.

You're the busiest bee in the hive.

Don't worry. I may be away from my desk but I'm thinking about work.

Let's get the company logo tattooed as a tramp stamp on our lower backs.

Make sure to remind the boss that he forgot to assign homework.

Have you thought of switching from work to, say, alcohol?

Do you sometimes wake up in the morning covered in paper cuts and files, unable to remember if you made any big sales the night before?

You must hate weekends.

Make sure to take time out of your work schedule today to just breathe.

John Calvin would be very proud of you.

It'll all pass soon.

Want a back rub?

Have you tried yoga? I did it once and hated it.

I think you're forgetting the company's golden rule: Fun comes first.

All you need is like 1,000 needles of acupuncture.

Stress is just your body telling you it hates you.

I would recommend dancing your stress away.

Would a Spanish poem help?

I heard that during World War II General Omar Bradley used to relax by doing calculus problems. Have you tried that?

I'm often reminded of what Winston Churchill said: "If you're going through hell, keep going."

You should meet my therapist, Dr. Jack Daniels.

Is now a bad time to talk with you about my personal problems?

Try taking deep breaths and punching a wall.

Is that one of those new Blackberry PDA wi-fi devices?

So you can check your email anywhere? Even in the bathroom?

Slow down. Your thumbs are smoking.

Did you get my email about you and me having a talk?

You sure do love your PDA, LOL.

I'll just wait until you're finished.

Some people think it's rude when people sit on their Blackberry when you're with them, but I actually take it as a really weird compliment that only the Blackberry and I understand.

All right, we get it—you have a friend who isn't us.

Jenga!

What's the latest on TMZ?

Have you reached level ten yet?

I just thought of the perfect birthday gift for you—a Blackberry-putter-away-er.

How long before your contract expires and you can get an iPhone?

# TO A COWORKER WHO IS ALWAYS ON THEIR PDA

You know we can see you and stuff, right?

During the rare times you're not using that, you should get a belt holster so it is available for quick access in times of crisis.

It's like your thumbs are tap dancing.

What's your highest score on that thing?

What do you pay for that every month in terms of friendships lost?

I'd get one of those, but I don't know Morse code.

It must be great that our bosses and clients can reach you 24 hours a day, seven days a week.

You must have been great at Asteroids as a kid.

So when was the last time you made eye contact with someone?

Your thumbs are going to be toast by the time you're 40.

Try up, down, up, down, b, a, b, a, select, start to get a free life.

This may seem weird, but I can't shake the urge to smash that with a hammer.

Wait—did you get an iPhone?

Tell me, is that like a great phone or the greatest phone?

Rumors are that Apple is going to release a new iPhone next week with everything not in the current model.

Does it cuddle?

Incredible engineering. Is it true you can watch YouTube videos?

What plan did you get?

Did I see you just update your Facebook page to say that right now you are talking to me about your iPhone?

I heard there's a website where you can hack your iPhone and hook it up to another service. All you need is a screwdriver, a soldering iron, some 18-gauge wire, epoxy and about three hours of free time.

Wanna see my Swiss Army knife?

I want it. Give it to me.

I'm going to go out, buy one and shove it in my grandpa's face.

It sure beats the heck out of relationships with actual people.

# TO A COWORKER WHO CAN TYPE REALLY FAST

Check out Type-y Gonzalez over here.

You ever enter any typing tournaments? I bet you'd do pretty well.

I think I see smoke coming off that keyboard.

It's like watching that dude from *Shine*.

When I watch you type it makes me wish that I too hadn't been good at sports.

You must be an absolute wiz at Donkey Kong.

Are you pushing all the buttons at once just to look cool?

It's like you invented typing or something.

Which is your favorite letter?

I want to see you race the fastest texter in the office.

So I assume you're doing a lot of blogging at home.

You're the man now, dog!

Slow down. Watching your fingers is going to drive me into a seizure.

Do you ice those fingers down at the end of the day?

# WHEN SOMEONE COMPLAINS OF CARPEL TUNNEL SYNDROME

You should try one of those wrist pads.

Maybe you should take it easy on the web surfing.

Don't play if you feel pain or else you could risk permanent injury.

You sure IMing to ten people in ten different windows at once isn't too much?

My grandpa had a hand injury years ago. His hand was crushed by an industrial metal press. Went back to work the next day.

Two words: heat and elevation. Thank me later.

How's the wrist holding up?

You may want to try a voice-activated computer typing program.

# "CAN YOU HELP ME WITH SOMETHING?"

I need to consult my Magic Eight Ball first.

You'll have to put your request in writing first.

Only if you pick me up at the airport on Sunday.

I don't think anyone can help you, buddy.

I can if you think I can.

I can probably pencil you in.

Sure. Have your people get ahold of my people.

Is it laundry?

Is this the "wink-wink, do you know a guy?" kind of help or the "which floor is accounting on?" kind of help?

Only if it's long and involved.

Sorry, I don't know anything about cars.

I'm not gonna lie—I'm not good at very many things.

Only if I get a back rub in return.

Is there a gold star in it for me?

Please see me after class.

You're grounded.

Don't worry, the meeting time I set up was just a suggestion.

You didn't miss much other than your colleagues sitting here waiting for you.

Sorry, but it's better if you leave.

We totally weren't talking about you before you got here.

Now that everyone's here, let's order lunch.

I told everyone you'd come, but nobody believed me.

Just as I suspected.

I could tell you that you missed something important, but come on—who are we kidding?

You can just listen to the podcast later.

We really didn't need you anyway.

We're already done.

Don't worry, you can borrow my notes later on.

# WHEN SOMEONE ASKS YOU A COMPUTER QUESTION

How could you work here and not know that?

Hold shift-alt-f7-control-option-delete-return-escape-tab-shift-tab-alt and press up arrow.

Do I look like I'm from a developing nation?

Do you have any idea how stupid that makes you sound?

Stay right here. I'm going for help.

That's hilarious. Wait. Are you serious?

Turn it off and on. After that, you're on your own.

I can help you with that, just as soon as I finish everything I'll ever have to do.

# TO A COWORKER WHO SENDS A LOT OF EMAIL FORWARDS

Hey, it's the Virus King!

Your last email forward didn't open, but I'll just wait for the next five.

I really get a kick out of those things, especially the really long ones.

I like how you start each email forward with "I know, I hate forwards too, but..." It's like you're doing a bit or something.

Can you just forward me the emails about cats?

I'm a few months behind on your forwards.

Another classic.

I didn't get a chance to read that because the company firewall blocked it.

I have to hook you up with my uncle Roger. He'd love you.

Something's wrong with my email. I keep setting your emails to spam, yet they keep coming through.

Nothing attached?

I don't read your emails because I'm swamped with actual work.

# TO A COWORKER WITH A REALLY MESSY DESK

FEMA called. They'd like their disaster back.

You're a real Messy Marvin.

Call in the excavation team, because I need to borrow a pen.

I think I see Jimmy Hoffa's toe sticking out.

Avalanche!

As long as you have a system, right?

I like this. It feels lived-in and homey.

But I bet at home you're a complete neat freak, am I right?

Did you do this in the hopes that someday soon there would be a messy desk calendar that you could try out for?

And there's a desk under there somewhere, right?

You should take a picture of your desk every day for a year, set it to music, and post it to YouTube.

Hey, I know everyone is always talking about your desk and how messy it is, but I just want you to know that I support you no matter what.

# TO A COWORKER WITH A REALLY CLEAN DESK

OCD much?

You're really making the rest of us look bad.

Hey, I know everyone's always talking about your desk and how weirdly clean it is, but I just want you to know that I think it's great and I support you no matter what.

Whoa! Is that a spit-shine on that puppy?

Do you have a maid?

There's a lot going on here.

I like the austere aesthetics of this desk.

You could eat off that desk. Though, then it'd be dirty. So maybe don't eat off it.

You know what they say: clean desk, dirty mind.

But no matter how clean you make your desk, there's still billions of bacteria that you can't see.

Twenty bucks says you're a big fan of hand sanitizer.

# "WHAT DID YOU DO LAST NIGHT?"

Stared at the walls.

Karate.

Math equations.

I had a date with Netflix.

Partied like a rock star.

I went on a 15-block pub crawl.

I inappropriately hit on the girl in the drive-thru.

I wish I could remember. Oh well, Percocet will do that.

I made a little progress on building a robot wife.

I got charged with resisting arrest for the hundredth time.

Rocked the mic.

The pet bear needed washing, so that was about it.

You may have noticed that the Joker didn't manage to poison the city's water supply last night. I hope that answers your question.

Well, let's just say it was either incredibly awesome or incredibly depressing.

# WHEN A COWORKER IS PLAYING MUSIC TOO LOUDLY

What band is that?

Have you ever tried those noise-canceling headphones? Those things are amazing.

I wasn't planning on getting any work done today anyway.

Is that freedom rock? Well then turn it up, man!

Let's start a mosh pit.

I admire your complete lack of concern for others' ability to concentrate.

Play whatever you want—just be sure to keep cranking it!

Hey, Casey Kasem—who's this song dedicated to?

Is that rap music?

I can really feel the music in my fillings.

# TO A COWORKER WHO SINGS ALL DAY LONG

You have a beautiful voice.

That's incredible. Thank you for sharing your gift with us.

And all that with no formal training, huh?

I used to sing, but somewhere along the way I lost my song.

Do you know "House of the Rising Sun?"

Did you do choir in school?

Ever cut an album?

Can you sing my outgoing voicemail message?

Ah, the dulcet sounds of work.

Instead of being here all day, you should be out recording an album.

Were your parents incredibly musical?

You should get a job at Google. There they tolerate this kind of crap.

Good stuff.

What's new in the funny pages today?

Uh oh, let me make sure my stitches are still attached.

Have you ever thought about trying to get an HBO special?

You have gotta start a blog.

No jokes today, please. My hernia's been acting up.

You have gotta take this act on the road.

I really like that you're able to be so hilarious without giving into the temptation to be salacious.

Laughter really is the best medicine.

When I first hear a good joke from you—that's when my work day really starts.

You got yourself a pretty a tight set.

You keep us laughing through the day.

You make me LOL.

# TO PEOPLE SMOKING OUT IN FRONT OF THE BUILDING

Didn't I see you guys out here yesterday?

You all look smoking!

Just between us, I think all those new cigarette taxes are a bunch of B.S.

Which of you has the most Marlboro Miles?

I'm a chewing tobacco man myself.

Raise your hand if you're "alive with pleasure."

Where my party people at?

Is used to smoke before the old ball-and-chain swiped my cigs.

Say what they may, you all get more fresh air than any of us inside.

I don't smoke, but I'd love to get in on this smoke break routine.

Hey, don't let Helen from the accounting department see you—she's super judgy about smoking.

A few more weeks at this job and I'll be right there with you.

I admire all of your perseverance.

# TO A COWORKER YOU CATCH DAYDREAMING

Wake up bro! You're not in Hawaii anymore.

Dreaming about buying a fishing boat off the coast of Italy?

Take me with you.

I remember what it was like to dream.

We're going to need you back here on planet Earth.

You're getting very slee-py...your eyes are growing hea-vy...

What was that waiter's name again? Oh that's right...Jean Luc.

Just whenever you have a minute.

You figure out the universe yet?

Don't worry, I'm sure you remembered to lock your door this morning.

Giselle or Shakira? McSteamy or McDreamy?

World Series, game seven, two outs, bottom of the ninth. He sees the pitch...it's back...and it's gone for a home run. Now get back to work.

Save the dreaming for the bathtub full of Calgon.

# TO A COWORKER YOU CATCH NAPPING

Take a minute.

You should open our new office in Madrid. You'd fit right in.

I see you've integrated lunch and sleep.

I understand Abe Lincoln was a big napper.

And how does this fit into your plan for world domination?

Were you having the dream where you show up to school naked and there's a test you didn't know about? I have that one all the time.

Were you having the dream where you show up to work and get caught napping? That would be super ironic if you were.

Kids keeping you up again?

Looks like someone's been partying too hard.

Those late nights will catch up with you.

Maybe you could share your thoughts on napping at the next shareholders meeting.

Is that the latest edition of Excel?

I like how you're crunching those numbers there.

That sure doesn't look like the Mackenzie proposal.

Look at that score. Now that's what I call exceeding the quarterly numbers.

Keep it up and we'll all be learning Chinese soon.

I heard this game got a really good review in *Bad Employee Monthly*.

Did you see that study that said playing video games at work makes people more efficient? Cause I didn't see it either.

And you wonder why all our jobs are going to India.

I got next.

I wish I had your guts. You're like Cool Hand Luke.

What do you do when the boss walks in?

So can I assume you've taken yourself out of the running for Employee of the Month?

## POWER PHRASES

### IT'S _____ TIME.

It's sandwich-artisting time.

It's drywall-hanging time.

It's sweater-folding time.

It's cold-calling time.

It's nodding-off-in-a-meeting time.

It's receipt-submitting time.

It's file-organizing time.

It's clocking-in time.

It's test-grading time.

It's toilet-plunging time.

It's parking ticket–writing time.

It's deposition-taking time.

# CHAPTER 3
# COWORKERS' PERSONAL LIVES

# WHEN A COWORKER TALKS ABOUT PERSONAL PROBLEMS ON THE PHONE

TMI.

Can you speak up? I can't hear all the little details I never wanted to hear.

I hope you don't mind, but I took notes.

Were you just on the phone with Dr. Phil?

I've got personal problems too, but I don't talk about them on the phone. That's what my blog is for.

Lot of information there.

Since I now know so much about you now, I feel I should share. I'm a polygamist.

That was all made up, right?

I feel like I finally understand you.

Someone needs a little vitamin H. (Open arms, offer hug.)

It's not your fault. It's your parents' fault.

You think you got problems? Don't get me started on my digestive problems.

I'm gonna get you the number to the Employee Assistance Program.

You should eat some fast food. The grease soaks up the alcohol.

If you really want to feel sick, you should take a look at the pile of work on your desk.

Seemed like a good idea last night.

You smell like my grandpa.

Have you tried a Bloody Mary?

You need a little hair of the dog.

Just like me back in my frat house days.

Let me guess, three too many?

If you're gonna throw up, do it behind the dumpster in the parking lot. Otherwise people will talk.

I hope you don't make everyone else in the office sick.

Long night?

You're glowing.

Saving on dry-cleaning, I see.

It's cool. I've been wearing the same underpants for a week straight.

I see you've gone to the uniform.

So I guess this means you've given up.

Hey, as long as you're changing your socks and underwear, I don't see a problem.

Did I ever tell you about the time I wore the same pair of jeans for six months?

# TO A COWORKER WHO JUST GOT A DUI

Are you going to fight it?

I bet you won't get more than a year with time off for good behavior.

Mind if I call you Dewey from now on?

How'd they catch you? Were you pouring beer out the window at a traffic light?

It's crazy, you only have to drink like six Long Island Iced Teas and you're over the limit.

Do you have to get one of those breathalyzers that won't let your car turn on if you're drunk?

You should have made a run for it.

Did you blow? The trick is to only pretend to blow.

Live and learn.

That's the price you pay to party.

You're going to come out of this a better person.

Just follow the program, bro.

I really admire what you're doing.

You're very courageous.

If you need me to bust you out, just say the word.

# MEANINGLESS ANSWERS TO COWORKERS' QUESTIONS

## "HOW ARE THE KIDS?"

Disappointing as ever.

They are divine. Seriously, I honestly think they're angels.

Turns out my son is actually a girl, so that's kind of surprising to find out after three years.

Did you talk to them?

I gotta be honest, they're kinda weirding me out.

I try not to think about them too much.

I'm pretty sure half of 'em have a serious drug habit.

Would you like to know alphabetically or sequentially? Either way, they're dumb.

I have a sneaky feeling they're up to something.

Secretive as ever.

I honestly could take 'em or leave 'em.

So f-ing great.

I try not to talk to them very much.

Your guess is as good as mine.

# TO A COWORKER WHO JUST GOT OUT OF REHAB

Good to have you back, bro.

Tell me all about the celebs you saw.

If you ever need to talk, please, feel free to get out of here and do so.

Welcome back to the world of the living.

I didn't even know you were gone.

So did you start smoking?

So what's Britney like?

What step are you on?

So no more partying for you? That sucks. We'll be thinking of you.

I guess I'll have to do all the drinking for both of us now.

# TO YOUR COWORKER WHO LOST A TON OF WEIGHT

You look great. Just great.

That's incredible. When I lost my weight it was with the help of a team of plastic surgeons.

How long till you put it all back on?

Now we can book the small conference room.

Wow, it's like you lost an entire family.

I always thought you made a nice husky person.

Did you buy all new jeans?

No more sweat stains on the chair for you.

I could never do what you did. Me, I just eat whatever I want and don't gain a pound.

Where did you go? You turned sideways and I lost track of you.

I'm definitely going to have to start sexually harassing you.

With so much less buoyancy, your bodysurfing skills probably won't be the same.

## TO A COWORKER WHO COMPLAINS ABOUT BEING SINGLE

It's tough out there.

Have you tried signing up for a cooking class?

You gotta be just so sick of the bar scene.

I'd set you up with someone, but all my friends are weird.

As soon as you stop looking, love will find you.

My grandparents met in a bar. Have you tried that yet?

But at least you're free to do what you want, when you want.

You don't need to conform to society's norm.

Maybe you should write to Oprah.

I heard you can buy all kinds of spouses from former Eastern Bloc countries.

Whatever you do, don't lower your standards.

I'll be honest, love is the one subject where I'm not an expert.

Sometimes I really think amoebas have it all figured out.

# TO A COWORKER WHO GETS ENGAGED

It's about time you settled.

Well, it was nice knowing you.

And they say online dating never works.

It's OK to consider this one a "starter marriage."

I see that accountant of yours finally talked a little sense into you.

And I always thought we had a chance, too.

Whatever you do, don't get married in a dormant volcano. My uncle found that out the hard way.

And there was absolutely no blackmail involved here, huh?

Now who asked whom?

Are you telling everyone yet or just me?

Are you thinking big wedding, small wedding or Vegas?

Have the lawyers hammered out the final agreement yet?

## "I'M HAVING SOME RELATIONSHIP PROBLEMS AND WOULD LIKE YOUR ADVICE."

If you follow my advice, you'll probably wind up living with your mom.

Yes. Don't get married.

Sure, but first you need to sign this release form.

You don't want me to whack them, do you?

What you need to do is to think with your heart.

Oh, I'm not sure you want my opinion or advice on anything of consequence.

What would happen if I just turned and ran away?

Sure. I don't have any formal counseling training, but I have a PhD in Failed Relationships.

Have you tried getting drunk before your dates?

Sure, but whatever you tell me, my advice will be the same: start binge drinking.

If it's anything other than a fight over what movie to see, I'm just about the last person you want to ask.

Of course. And let's hug afterward.

# TO SOMEONE COLLECTING FOR A COWORKER'S WEDDING GIFT

Thanks, but I already got them nothing.

Can't we just get them one of those homemade gift certificates for free back rubs?

I'm not sure they're really expecting anything.

Won't a gift send the wrong message?

Let's step back from the ledge here and really think about this.

This could set a dangerous precedent.

I've got fifty cents for a card.

I know for a fact she hates gifts.

Let's make a gift from items in the supply closet. It will mean so much more.

Can I keep the receipt? I'm having some tax issues.

Do you need a blank check or should I just take $300 out at the ATM?

I'm in if the gift is a gift of friendship.

# TO A COWORKER WHO GETS A MAIL-ORDER BRIDE

I can't believe you told us you got a mail-order bride.

Does she speak any English yet or still just Russian?

I hope their customer service is better than ours.

I bet that set you back a pretty penny.

Is she tax deductible?

You're desperate but practical. That's what I admire about you.

Remember what they say: you're not just marrying her—you're marrying her entire family.

Hope you like borscht.

You look like an entirely different person.

You're glowing.

I wish I could see your wedding photos, but I'm highly allergic to the chemicals they use to process them.

Did you save me some cake?

Here's comes the bride!

How many blenders did you get?

So...you gonna stay together?

Sure was nice of Oprah to pay for the whole thing.

Now comes the fun part: writing the thank you notes.

I still have six months to get you a gift, right?

I heard the wedding was a lot of fun too.

How's domestic bliss treating you?

I've heard that wherever it was you went on your honeymoon is just amazing.

# TO A COWORKER RETURNING FROM A HONEYMOON

Well, while you two were watching the surf and sipping tropical drinks, I was stuck here in the office drinking tropical-themed drinks under my desk.

How was Niagara Falls?

So did you get lucky?

Congratulations. I just saw on the news that over 47 percent of married couples get divorced before the honeymoon is over.

On my honeymoon the better half and I just locked ourselves in my folks' basement with twelve cases of Pabst Blue Ribbon. Best week of my life.

So when am I going to get some grandkids out of the two of you?

# TO COWORKER WHO IS PREGNANT

When's the due date?

Girl or boy?

You are totally glowing.

You're gonna be an awesome mom.

Are you still pregnant?

Pick out any names yet?

Are you going to be one of those "cool moms" or one of those "super strict moms"?

Any cravings?

Are you going to take any maternity leave?

I'll try to keep my secondhand smoke away from you and your unborn baby.

Is the baby behaving so far?

I'm not going to lie—I'm afraid of babies.

Your accountant must be so excited.

I'm just throwing this out there: Randy makes a great name for both a boy or a girl.

# TO A COWORKER WHO JUST HAD A BABY

Is that a family name or just something special you picked out?

So you're probably not sleeping much these days.

The first six weeks are the toughest.

Having fun yet?

It's truly life's greatest blessing.

This is one of the few things in life you can't undo.

This is gonna put a kink in the old sleeping schedule.

Is he a good sleeper?

What's been the biggest surprise so far?

You should email all of us some pictures.

Is she colicky?

Does she know any tricks yet?

Just remember not to throw the baby out with the bath water.

Who else is pitching in?

We should check to see if she's registered anywhere.

Are you sure about this?

How do we know what the baby wants?

As long as I don't have to go make the purchase, I'm down.

Is she still pregnant?

I vote for getting a set of antique dueling pistols.

Maybe we could draw some certificates good for a free hour of babysitting.

Too bad we can't give her an entire night's sleep.

That's a great idea. I know I sure appreciated that present you all got for me when I adopted that foster kid. Oh wait, that never happened.

Whatever we get, let's be sure it's not made in China.

## MEANINGLESS ANSWERS TO COWORKERS' QUESTIONS

# "WHO ARE YOU VOTING FOR?"

As a convicted felon, I'm forbidden from voting.

Reagan-Bush '80!

I believe it's "For *whom* are you voting?"

How about you tell me who you're voting for so I can do the opposite?

Guess I'll be choosing the lesser of two evils, right?

Whoever is taller.

Whoever takes a harder line on parking tickets.

I'm going to write in Obama for every office from now on. That's how much meaning his election gave to my otherwise vapid existence.

It's like choosing who you want to rob you—am I right?

I always write in Batman.

After I tell you, can we talk about our religious beliefs?

I wish you were running, because you'd be my candidate.

Whoever promises more free stuff from the government.

# TO A COWORKER WHO BRINGS THEIR KIDS INTO WORK

Careful—two more visits and your kids get a cubicle and time cards.

Do you want me to pretend like you're really important when your kids are around?

Have they had all their shots?

I know you don't steal office supplies—but your kids are stealing office hearts.

How do they take their coffee?

Finally—someone who can tell us what to do here.

Can we teach them to collate?

Oh, to be young again.

Does this mean we get nap time today?

You don't by chance have an extra juice box, do you?

Any imaginary friends get left at home today?

Finally a chance to get caught up on the filing.

In some parts of the world they'd be getting paid to be here.

Get used to it kids, 'cause this is the rest of your life.

How about they do some of my work and I go outside and play.

They have your eyes. And ability to close a deal.

Did the nanny get deported?

Are these cursing-friendly kids or should I watch my mouth?

I wish I could see my cost analysis reports through their eyes.

I'm looking at America's most precious natural resource... children.

Nice to see someone with brains in this office.

Think of me as the uncle/aunt who really likes it quiet. Are we getting each other?

I can't wait until they grow up.

When do they start being interesting?

So, you have to go home to that?

Let's find out how many times I can spin them around before they fall down.

# ON TAKE YOUR DAUGHTER TO WORK DAY

I was going to bring my daughter in, but she hates me.

I bet she'll be running this place in a couple of years.

This is where daddy comes to die.

My daughter doesn't even know where I work.

Oh dear. Did I forget my daughter again this year?

Who approved all this?

This is all part of the national effort to demoralize girls from as young an age as possible.

I just barely got all my Take Your Daughters To Work Day cards in the mail on time this year.

I think a little Double Dutch would do wonders for corporate morale.

Time held me green and dying, though I sang in my chains like the sea.

Put me down for the least tacky item.

Of course! What are coworkers for?

Sure, I'll buy a few things to avoid your hateful glare.

Support the Girl Scouts? I'm not sure how I feel about that issue.

What's the least expensive thing?

And these are competitive rates for scented candles?

I love buying things and then three months later I get a surprise delivery of things I forgot I wanted.

Oh, great. And tomorrow I'd like to chat with your about a timeshare I'm buying in Jamaica.

Now is this pro-children or anti-children? 'Cause I'm still not sure where I come down on that issue.

Time to treat myself right.

This will arrive in time for the company Secret Santa, right?

# TO A COWORKER WHO JUST GOT DIVORCED

Hang in there, bro.

Hang in there, girl.

Just think, by the time next Olympics roll around, you'll feel much better.

Let your job help you through this. Why don't you start by copying and collating this for me?

Tell me you had a prenup.

I have an old toaster you can have.

When I broke up with my girlfriend at the start of summer vacation in 4th grade, I was miserable for days.

Have you tried lap dance therapy yet?

What you need is a Mustang convertible.

Elizabeth Taylor has been divorced like eleven times, and she's honestly one of the happiest people I know.

The best thing to do in this situation is the drink away the next six months.

# WHEN YOU BUMP INTO A COWORKER OUTSIDE OF WORK

Hi. (Keep walking.)

You never saw me.

What's been going on since I saw you at work today?

Now we both know what the other one wears when we're not in the office.

Wanna exchange phone numbers?

Wow. This feels like bumping into one of my teachers at the grocery store.

Did you get time off for good behavior?

I hardly recognized you when you're not sitting behind a giant stack of papers.

I always assumed you lived at the office.

How'd you escape?

Wanna agree to never speak of this ever again?

## WHEN YOU BUMP INTO TWO COWORKERS WHO ARE CLEARLY ON A DATE

Hi. (Keep walking.)

Great to see you guys.

BUS-TED!

Did you see the latest Hanson proposal? Crazy, right?

Awk-ward.

So that's why you would never go out with me.

You guys are really committed to your work.

Your secret is safe with me.

Who's putting this on the corporate account?

Believe me, I wanted this to happen even less than you did.

I'll get you those figures first thing Monday.

Let's just quickly fist bump and I'll get out of here.

## "ARE YOU SEEING ANYONE?"

My therapist won't let me.

Don't you hate that term—"seeing" someone? Since when does dating involve stereoscopic vision?

Nah. My wives keep running out on me.

Can't afford it.

I've been trolling Craigslist for weeks, but no luck yet.

I wish.

First I'm going to have to deal with several of my severe phobias.

It's hard to meet people who don't ask too many questions.

I was, but apparently I'm "extremely ugly" to the "opposite gender."

Why? Do you have some sister that got kicked in the head by a horse or something?

I'm dating a supermodel in Belgium, but don't try to look her up on the Internet or anything because she's not on the Internet.

It's hard for me to date because I love so much.

# WHEN YOU BUMP INTO A COWORKER AT THE MALL

Hi. (Keep walking.)

Are you following me?

I have never felt so uncomfortable.

Wanna talk about work?

So you don't go into the office on the weekends? Me neither.

Please tell me there's not a sales meeting in the food court.

Picking up some new Dockers?

What have you been doing since I last saw you five minutes ago?

Do you want to head down to the Cinnabon and get a jump start on the new presentation?

Since we're both here, should we just pick out each other's gift for Secret Santa?

If I bump into you in my living room next, I'm really going to freak out.

# TO DECLINE A COWORKER'S PARTY INVITATION

I have a dentist appointment.

I wish I could come, but I'm putting the final touches on my novel.

I would be there, but my new parole officer is a real hard ass.

Our regular sitter is out of town.

I really don't do well in crowds.

I can't. I'm what some would call a "problem" drinker.

I have other plans already. I'm serious.

Is it a swingers party? My wife/husband is a freak! Otherwise, no thanks.

My husband and I are doing some canning that night. Strawberry preserves.

I want to, but we can't get that close. It's complicated. (Run off.)

# AT YOUR BOSS' BIRTHDAY PARTY

She should be buying us presents, right?

We really need to rehearse before we sing "Happy Birthday."

I heard there's an after party in accounting.

Let's all chip in and not buy him a gift.

Is it wrong to regift the uninteresting present he got us for our birthdays?

Do you think it was inappropriate to give her a card that said "Happy Birthday. In lieu of a gift, I've donated my life to making you look good"?

Who brought our list of demands?

Who wants to be the first to leave?

All I ask is that we don't fake smile for a group photo.

Does a paper cup full of cheap champagne seem oddly appropriate to anyone else?

I've heard so many nice things about you.

It is so nice to meet you, and I'm not just saying that because your husband does my performance reviews.

You should see his office—it's covered in pictures of you.

You look luminous.

How did you two meet?

Where are you from originally?

I feel like I know you already.

Could you imagine if you and I exchanged notes? He would be in deep trouble.

I'll keep an eye on him for you.

Have you been introduced to his "work wife"?

Does she boss you around, too?

How did you two kids meet?

You did good for yourself, fella.

She really is a great boss, isn't she?

You and I should start some kind of support group.

So you're not one of those house husbands are you?

Are you doing enough to keep a stress-free environment at home?

You may be the only person in this world who understands what my life is like.

So what was the interview process like for you?

She goes on and on about you all the time.

It's nice to finally put a face to the name. Now which of her two husbands are you?

# POWER PHRASES

## YOU'RE THE ____ OF ____.

You're the Michael Jordan of editorial writing.

You're the Tiger Woods of the Bloody Mary.

You're the Bill Gates of canned tomato processing.

You're the Albert Einstein of tour-giving.

You're the Secretariat of auto detailing.

You're the Herbert Hoover of birthday party clowns.

You're the Stephen Spielberg of dental x-rays.

You're the Gregory Hines of the audit.

You're the Harry Houdini of mileage logs.

You're the Rembrandt of the leafblower.

You're the Jackson Pollock of electrolysis.

# CHAPTER 4
# COWORKERS' HOBBIES AND OBSESSIONS

Hey slugger.

Quite a game yesterday.

Watching the game tonight?

No harm, no foul.

You should be the GM for a baseball team.

I think the team is going all the way this year.

How many points did the Yankees score yesterday?

Let's get season tickets to the ballet...I mean the Bears.

I wish the players on my fantasy team would start scoring.

I think we're two years away from a championship.

When are they firing the coach already?

Pete Rose—in or out?

How about that WNBA?

What's your favorite sports metaphor?

Eight gold medals in one Olympics. Michael Phelps—the greatest athlete of all time. End of story.

You know, back in the day I was getting looked at pretty seriously by some pro scouts.

We should be allowed to wear our favorite team's jersey to the office.

I agree with George Will that football combines the two worst things about America: violence punctuated by committee meetings.

Looks like you could use some relief from the bullpen.

We should dump a bucket of Gatorade over the boss' head.

No sliding head first into the desk, OK?

Want to come over to my house and watch the big game? And by big game I mean my dog cleaning his rear with his tongue.

I keep hearing that soccer is the sport of the future.

You know, Tiger Woods seems pretty good to me.

The best thing about the Super Bowl is the commercials.

I'm thinking about naming my daughter Favrette.

Can you explain what a sports hernia is?

# TO A COWORKER WHO IS REALLY INTO THEIR CATS

What a regal animal.

Which is the one that thinks it's a person?

And did you name all of them?

They look like a real handful.

How many lives does this one have left?

In ancient Egypt, cats were worshipped as gods.

Ever wonder what they think about all day?

Do they know any tricks?

I knew someone who had cats once.

I bet they each totally have their own unique personality.

All of your cat sweaters really brighten my day, particularly those with puffy paint.

So catnip is basically just feline heroin, right?

Is your cat totally the boss of your house?

I like these cat pictures, but I'd love to see some pictures of your spouse and children.

# TO A COWORKER WHO IS REALLY INTO THEIR CATS

I often read about how independent cats are. Care to confirm?

What's the absolutely cutest thing it's ever done?

Do they still make Tender Vittles?

Something about kitty noses makes me happy.

Do they ever try to eat you?

I love cats, especially with a little garlic and mashed potatoes.

Do you ever walk them on a leash?

They say cats are much more closely related to lions than dogs are to wolves.

Hang in there!

You know, this researcher at 0.–San Francisco found a link between cats and schizophrenia. It has something to do with the toxoplasma parasite that cats carry. He found the link in the brain slices of schizophrenics, many of whom, statically, grew up with cats. Anyway, it's really interesting. You should check it out sometime when your cats are out of town.

Don't you love that new car smell?

Good week at the track?

When can I borrow it?

How many cup holders?

I heard those got a really good review in *Consumer Reports*.

Does it get better mileage then your old Hummer?

Did you spring for the sport package?

I guess someone's rich uncle died. Oh he really did? My bad. Sorry for your loss.

Let's take it to lunch and flip off those jerks from accounting.

We're still going to hang out now, right?

It's nice, but there's no way you have anywhere near the storage space as my mini-van.

I was going to get a new car too, but I'd much rather pay off student loans.

Have you really opened it up yet?

You should get insurance for this one.

# TO A COWORKER WHO JUST BOUGHT A NEW CAR

How long do you think it'll work?

As soon as you drive it off the lot, it loses something like 98 percent of its value.

Do you think this will finally help you make friends?

They saw you coming a mile away.

Did you get a driver too?

I'll race you.

I have that same car in my Matchbox collection.

Hey there, Mr. Vroom Vroom.

So how does it work?

# TO A COWORKER WHO JUST BOUGHT A HOUSE

I heard that buying a house is the best investment you can make.

You're living the American Dream.

Did you see the front page story in yesterday's *Wall Street Journal*?

Are you doing any work on it?

Is the outhouse close by?

Which of the rooms is your favorite?

Don't forget to invite everyone to the housewarming party.

I'm very uncomfortable with this conversation. My great-aunt was the Wicked Witch of the East.

Did the movers break anything?

Can I come over and borrow the hot tub?

How's the water pressure?

Who did you have to kill to get approved for a mortgage?

Did it come with a moat or are you gonna put one in later?

Don't forget to get flood insurance.

# TO A COWORKER WHO IS INTO HIGH-TECH GADGETS

I heard a rumor that there's a new iPhone with everything coming out soon.

I bet you have a laserdisc player.

Blu-ray, shmoo-ray.

How many little pixies does your HDTV have?

I'm always amazed at how technology enriches our lives.

Have you heard about those new pills that you just add water and they turn into a steak?

I'm still learning to use DOS.

So what's your favorite toy?

You buy a new computer—bam!—a month later it's completely obsolete.

I'm thinking about making my grandma's lasagna recipe "open-source."

I bet you'd be able to fix my VCR so it wasn't flashing "12:00" all day.

Do you Linux?

# TO A CIGAR-OBSESSED COWORKER

I heard Cubans are the best.

Ever get any Cubans?

Besides Cuba, where do good cigars come from?

I saw that Cuba recently set the record for the world's longest cigar.

Cigars add a touch of class to any setting. Especially Cubans.

When you smoke a Cuban, does it just make all other cigars seem silly by comparison?

I heard you can get Cubans in Canada.

I think Cubans are the best because of something to do with the soil that they grow the tobacco in.

Do you have a humidor? Is that where you keep your Cubans?

Do you think in Cuba they call Cuban cigars "cigars"?

## MEANINGLESS ANSWERS TO COWORKERS' QUESTIONS

## "WHAT DO YOU DO FOR FUN?"

Extra work.

Lots of eating.

Push-ups.

Update my blog.

I'm really into archery.

I'll let you know when I figure it out.

Various humanitarian efforts.

Civic activities.

I think about what animals are doing.

I panic.

Go to my therapist.

I'm building a bunker.

Let's just say that I'm a bit of a foodie.

Whatever seems most faddish at the time.

Which one of your guns are you going to use when you become a disgruntled former employee?

Do you give your guns lady names?

Which is the gun you sleep with under your pillow?

I'm looking to buy a Barrett for deer hunting.

What I'm interested in is stopping power.

I'm more of a crossbow guy.

We should head out to the old rail yard one weekend and shoot up some cans.

Do you have any extra NRA bumper stickers I can have? I feel like that might help me with tailgaters.

Let me know if you ever have any trouble getting any of your meds.

When civilization collapses, can I crash at your place?

Huh.

# WHEN SOMEONE IS REALLY INTO THE ENVIRONMENT

Did you know there are over 200 uses for hemp?

The environment is such a good cause.

It's like, when will we start respecting the Earth?

Can I recycle these old pencil shavings?

I've got an inconvenient truth for you: I need a cocktail.

I hope your efforts cancel out mine.

We only have one Earth, you know?

I try to throw out only garbage and stuff I don't want anymore.

If you can get our boss to cut down on some of the hot air, that would be a good way to fight global warming.

But I can't do anything about the environment. I'm just one person.

Think globally, act cubically.

# TO A COWORKER WHO TRIES TO SIGN YOU UP FOR A CHARITY

I'm not nuts about charity. It just seems so condescending.

I can't donate till I pay off my student loans.

All my charity work goes to the FDNY and PETA.

Can I just give you some old pants or some cans of refried beans?

If you want charity, you should see my apartment.

My charity is the LA Clippers. (Or Kansas City Royals.)

I give till it hurts, and right now I'm in agonizing pain.

What do I get out of the deal?

I'll do your charity with you if you help me with my charity next week. It's a program to give prostate exams to needy bulls.

I just got hit with a big IRS penalty, so things are really tight for me right now.

I just saw a *60 Minutes* report linking that charity to al-Qaeda.

# TO SOMEONE WHO HAS A LOT OF PICTURES ON THEIR DESK

So that's your family...

You have a great eye.

A lot of good times there.

Are these digital prints?

Any wacky family shots?

And which of these are Photoshopped?

Those pictures must remind you why we work as hard as we do.

If you ever forget what your relatives look like, you must be really glad to have these here.

I hate to be the one to tell you this, but you are very telegenic.

Those are all worth at least a thousand words.

I hope you have pictures of us on your desk at home.

# WHEN SOMEONE IS SHOWING YOU PICTURES FROM THEIR EXOTIC VACATION

Wow.

Looks beautiful.

I saw a show about that place on the Travel Channel.

That's you?

You gotta give me the name of your travel agent.

You're a real globe trotter. Not the basketball kind.

Good for you for doing that.

Next time, take me with you.

Thanks for not inviting me.

How many more pictures of unique flowers do you have?

I can't look anymore—I'm just too jealous.

I can't believe you came back.

Well, cookies for you.

Can you just send me the link when you put them up online?

## MEANINGLESS ANSWERS TO COWORKERS' QUESTIONS

# "WANNA HIT THE GYM LATER?"

Sure. I'll bring the smokes.

Why? Do you think my lats are looking a little husky these days?

Only if I have time to load up on protein shakes first.

And then we would work out together, or what?

I'd rather you didn't see me sweat.

Sorry friend. I work without a spotter.

Is that code for going on a bender? Because if that's the case, then yes, yes, yes.

How many reps are we looking at?

You know how they say not to mix business and pleasure? I don't know what this counts as, but it's probably a really bad thing for coworkers to do together.

I'm practically naked when I work out, and I don't think my coworkers should see me like that.

I'm already headed home for 100 Budweiser curls.

You don't get a body like this by going to the gym.

# TO A COWORKER WHO EATS ETHNIC FOODS

Is that what they call a hamburger in your homeland?

That looks way better than a turkey sandwich.

Who needs a personality when you can eat that?

I love the smell of fermented beans in the morning.

You'd love this great Antarctican restaurant in my neighborhood.

I have a great paprika guy if you want his info.

Did you lose some kind of bet?

Have you seen my cat?

I love that smell. Reminds me of the paper mill where my father used to work.

Well, aren't you just cutting edge.

# TO A COWORKER WHO EATS HEALTH FOODS

Are you sure that's safe?

You're becoming more and more like Oprah every day.

That has been scientifically proven to improve both circulation and how much of a hippie you are.

Soy lowers your sperm count. Just an FYI.

I ate seaweed once. That was all the health food I'll ever need.

I rather eat like a lion than a bunny.

And somehow eating this stuff makes you healthier or something?

This must be fun for your loved ones.

I'm with you. My body is a temple. Temple of Doom!

I eat only superfoods. Almonds, salmon, broccoli, Play-doh, Everlasting Gobstoppers.

That's why you have such beautiful skin and nails.

Have you tried that new Two Buck Chuck? It only cost two dollars, but it's supposed to be the best wine on the market.

Did you know escargot are actually snails?

What is the most memorable meal you've ever had? Please, tell us about it in detail.

You must love Red Lobster.

I know a place that serves the best food.

You must be a great treasure to take to a normal restaurant.

I prefer to find other things to be pretentious about.

To me, food is just fuel. Nothing more, nothing less.

Have you ever had that sushi that will kill you if the chef makes the slightest mistake?

What's up, Wolfgang Puck?

# WHEN A COWORKER WANTS TO TALK ABOUT A NEW MOVIE RELEASE

So how many thumbs do you give it?

Did you get popcorn?

Is that the one with Christopher Walken?

Don't tell me. I'm saving that one for my spouse.

I see movies only on IMAX. It's my thang.

Any nudity?

How were the special effects?

Just tell everyone what happens at the end so we can all save ten bucks.

You should write review movies for the local paper.

Did you buy your tickets online? I hear that's a breeze.

Was it a talkie?

I gotta tell ya, I'm more a TV person.

I went to the movies once.

Adjusted for inflation, movie tickets are cheaper now than during the Great Depression.

## MEANINGLESS ANSWERS TO COWORKERS' QUESTIONS

# "WANNA SEE MY NEW TATTOO?"

Is it the Chinese symbol for integrity? I've already seen fifty of those.

Oh, you got a new one?

Nothing I'd rather do than see your skin with a drawing on it.

Is it permanent?

Let's get ink'd!

Sure. Let's step into the restroom.

Is it stupid? Wait, don't answer that.

Is it your baby mama's name?

Is it one of the permanent ones?

Did you know that John Popper of Blues Traveler has a tattoo across his chest that says "I want to be brave"?

OK, and if you have the same thing as my uncle, don't worry because I won't tell him.

Depends. Was alcohol involved?

# WHEN EVERYONE IS TALKING ABOUT THE SAME TV SHOW

Are you guys talking about *Lost*?

Sorry—I don't own a TV.

I prefer to wait for it to come out in book form.

I'm more of a reader.

Don't tell me...I still don't know who shot J.R.

It's times like these I really regret shooting my TV with a revolver.

And then what happened?

If it's not on PBS, I don't watch it.

I only watch British comedies.

I'll just Netflix the whole season next year and watch it all in one night.

Is that a cable show or something? Never heard of it.

I've haven't seen a single episode, but I don't want it ruined for me in case I do.

Are there clips of it on YouTube?

Did you see it in HD?

# TO COWORKERS TALKING ABOUT AMERICAN IDOL

Let's keep our relationship on a professional level.

Don't tell me. I haven't caught up since Season Two. I think Clay Aiken is going to win.

You know who my American idol is? You.

Can I still try out this year?

I wish our boss was a lot more Randy and a lot less Paula.

I never watch television. I'm a reader.

I didn't catch last night's *American Idol* because I have friends and a social life.

I've never heard of it.

I love that show, except that Banker is so mean.

Did anyone sing "The Greatest Love of All" last night?

Who did you vote for?

That Simon can be a real jerk.

Don't you like it when Randy calls people "dawg"?

# POWER PHRASES

## LET'S GET OUR _____ HEADS IN THE _____ GAME.

Let's get our book-publishing heads in the book-publishing game.

Let's get our real estate appraisal heads in the real estate appraisal game.

Let's get our vending machine heads in the vending machine game.

Let's get our firefighting heads in the firefighting game.

Let's get our drink-mixing heads in the drink-mixing game.

Let's get our fashion design heads in the fashion design game.

Let's get our career counselor heads in the career counseling game.

# CHAPTER 5

# STRESSFUL MOMENTS
# AT WORK

Stay strong.

Hold your head up.

Don't let them drag you down.

Keep on truckin'.

Keep hope alive.

Don't stop believin'.

You're an inspiration to us all.

Don't give up now.

You'll make it through.

Oprah believes in you.

You'll be all right.

Everything will work out in the end.

Keep the faith.

Proud to know you.

Keep fighting the good fight.

Fight fire with fire.

Don't quit on us.

Be brave.

Tomorrow's another day.

Keep moving forward.

Once more unto the breach, dear friends.

It's bound to get better.

You're due.

I'm proud of you for trying.

You're gonna be OK on this one.

Just keep that fire burning.

All you can do is try.

You've got the touch. You've got the power.

Don't lose heart.

Keep your head down and just keep pushing forward.

You've nothing to fear but fear itself.

Keep doing what you're doing.

It could always be worse.

Focus on the positive.

You'll definitely come out stronger on the other end.

Give it a little time.

Keep doing what works.

Don't forget to keep things real.

You should be all right.

I'm worried about you, but I know you're strong.

Remember that the Chinese word for "problem" is the same as the word for "opportunity."

As Chairman Mao was fond of saying, "It's always darkest before it's totally black."

# "HOW'S THAT NEW PROJECT COMING ALONG?"

That's highly confidential.

I would tell you, but I'd have to kill you.

What new project?

Who told you about that?

I don't want to ruin my big presentation for you.

This is the one that puts us on the map.

Oh, it's gonna be big. Very big.

Let's just say that you're gonna freak.

Oh, it's gonna be a game changer.

It's generating a lot of buzz.

It's got an ETA of infinity.

Let's just say that it's going to shake everything up.

Can't say. I'm more of a "swoop in and take the credit" guy than a "get my hands dirty" guy.

It will make you question everything.

Prepare to have your socks knocked off.

# WHEN SOMEONE HAS A TERRIBLE IDEA

I like it—it just seems "off-brand."

How does that square with our core synergies?

Let's keep churning here.

I'm not sure we're there yet.

Might be something of a hard sell.

You might want to play that one close to your vest.

Welcome to Bad Idea City, USA. Population: You.

That dog don't hunt. I'm not sure it even goes outside that often.

Let's not just think outside the box here. Let's physically tie the box to a Hummer and drive it into the ocean.

I like that. I really do. I really, really, really do. But I just don't see it ever happening.

Let's just keep that one between you and me.

We might have to send that idea back for more testing.

Wait, did we want this to work or is that sort of unimportant at this stage?

Well, good luck cleaning yourself with that washcloth.

The only problem is that we're in the business of making money.

Hold off a second on that one—we haven't gotten to the bad ideas yet.

Let's remember that there are no bad ideas, but rather just bad employees.

We may have to dock you a week's pay.

That bear ain't got shoulders to pin.

The only bad ideas are that one and any like it.

The good thing about that idea is it lets us know what we shouldn't do.

That idea's going to end up on your permanent record.

Now's when you should throw a smoke bomb and disappear.

What else you got, General Custer?

Let's take that idea and run with it into the trash bin.

I like that. It's like a worse mousetrap. Genius.

# WHEN SOMEONE HAS A TERRIBLE IDEA

And you're really not horsing around right now?

You might want to workshop that a bit before bringing it to the group.

Wow. And people make fun of New Coke.

You can't make a purse out of a sow's ear.

That's what you call a no-brainier.

Maybe in France.

Save that for your next job.

There go our bonuses.

All right, good. Now let's move on to the real ideas.

An idea man you are not.

Did you just quit on me?

OK...let's start this meeting from the beginning.

We don't even have to vote on that one.

Is it me or did you just say something really funny?

Let's shelve that one forever.

# WHEN YOU'RE PRAISED FOR YOUR WORK

Well, let's not go crazy here.

All right, that's enough already.

I got lucky on that one.

Even though I did all the work myself, it was a team effort.

Even though I know you're lying, I appreciate it.

I'm sure I'll screw something up soon and balance it out.

Well, I must say, flattery will get you everywhere.

Sorry, I'm taken.

I'd feel more comfortable if you were just screaming at me like my father.

Are you looking to borrow money or something?

# WHEN YOU EXCEED YOUR SALES GOALS

That's what I do.

I smell a pizza party.

Now what?

I guess I'll be playing quite a bit of golf on company time next quarter.

Never had a doubt in my mind.

I laugh at your mortal sales goals.

Could've gone bigger but I figured, hey, leave something for the rest of the guys.

GOOOOOOOOOOOOOOOOOOOOAL!

I think the most important part is not that I made my goals, but that I had fun doing it.

You can all find out how I did it next Saturday during my seminar at the Airport Hilton.

I'm good. I worked hard and I won.

Isn't that what we're supposed to do?

# WHEN YOU FAIL TO MEET YOUR SALES GOALS

I hope they don't send a note to my parents, or I'm busted.

There goes the family vacation.

I don't measure success in dollars and cents.

So it was a Cadillac, a set of steak knives...what was third place again?

I thought we called them goals because they're completely unattainable.

The important thing is that we learned something.

I set my own goals to determine whether I'm a success or not.

Let's not start blaming each other.

Let's find the silver lining to this cloud.

Well, let's not beat ourselves up over it.

I always thought our number one goal was to have fun.

We may not have made our sales goals, but our expense accounts far exceeded expectations.

It's the economy, stupid.

We have sales goals?

# TO A PROSPECTIVE CLIENT

You complete me.

Let's not think about this as "you and me." Let's think about this as "us."

Think of my company as the person you had a crush on in high school who would never talk to you. That's what we can give you.

If we don't make this deal happen, I'm going to flip out. Seriously.

This could be the greatest day of your life.

You know you're my dawg, right?

My company is Zan. Your company is Jana. Now let's get together and form an eagle and a bucket of water.

I'm just going to have to insist that you trust me on this one.

You don't yank my chain, I won't yank yours. Deal?

I didn't want to say anything, but I spent this commission already, so you kind of owe this to me.

Way to go team! We just landed the trophy fish!

Way to go team! Just let's take a moment to appreciate our accomplishment.

Way to go team! Totally a team effort.

Way to go team! Let's hope we get through a few billing cycles before they figure out that we have no idea what we're doing.

Way to go team! Guess someone must have had some incriminating photographs, huh?

Way to go team! I finally feel like a complete person.

Way to go team! But keep in mind that if this new client is so great, how could they possibly be dumb enough to do business with us?

Way to go team! Now we'll finally get the respect we deserve.

Way to go team! Does this mean we can finally lose the old clients we secretly hate?

## MEANINGLESS ANSWERS TO COWORKERS' QUESTIONS

## "WHAT'S GOING ON IN YOUR DEPARTMENT?"

Lots.

Business is being done.

I try not to ever know.

We've been subverting the dominant paradigm.

That's a great question.

I wish I knew.

I hoped you were going to tell me.

Just ducking and diving.

Our new manager is a real piece of work.

Same as it ever was.

Just trying to keep our heads down.

We continue to find out different ways not to do things.

Everyone's getting along great and people are working in harmony toward a common goal.

We're thinking of buying a goat as a mascot.

We're working on something big. Real big.

# WHEN THE NEW SALES PITCH BOMBS

Well, that went well.

It's their loss.

We didn't want to do business with them anyway.

Some people just don't get it.

So that just happened.

I need a drink.

I don't think that was as bad as it seemed.

Excuse me, I have to call my wife and tell her to stop payment on the new Sea-Doos.

That was all courtesy of the Good Idea Fairy.

Quick, let's lock ourselves in the panic room.

They'll be back.

I didn't see that coming.

Did someone get the license plate on that bus?

Well, I guess I'm moving back into my mom's basement.

# AFTER YOUR TEAM FINISHES A BIG PROJECT

Now all we have to do is wait for management to come in and screw it up.

I think we've all earned some serious online crossword puzzle time.

Oh no. Did anyone spell check the document?

I think I'm all set in the actual "working" department for the year now.

I say we delete the whole thing and start from scratch.

I don't want to jinx anything, but I'm feeling a home run on this one.

Where should we put it for safekeeping?

Now let's start bickering over who did what.

Good luck getting me to do any work the rest of the week.

This could be the Big One, fellas.

If this doesn't land us the account, nothing will.

Can I just say one thing? It's been a pleasure!

I guess we should just start the weekend now.

# TO A COWORKER ON A BUSINESS TRIP

Wanna communicate only with text messages until we get home?

What color rental car do you think we'll get?

I've heard there's some good hiking where we're headed.

I'm writing a letter. I'm going to give it to you, and if anything happens to me I want you to give it to my wife.

Here we are, just like old times.

How many socks are you bringing?

Did you remember your passport?

FYI—when I'm on the road, I'm not a big shower-and-deodorant guy.

Let's try to set aside some time to sample the local cheeses.

Any interest in a brewery tour?

Can I have your aisle seat? I'm what doctors call a "puker."

Do you know of any good escort services where we're headed?

I have a whole other second wife and kids in this town that know nothing about my family back home. So if you bump into them, play it cool.

Let's pretend we're CIA assassins this week. Whadya say, Agent Black?

You're going to see some serious fudging of my expense account this week, and I just want to know if you're down for the cause.

I love business travel. I guess I'm just a sucker for hotel chicken fingers.

We owe it to ourselves to get up super early tomorrow and see some of the sights around town.

Wanna see if we can get bunk beds?

Can you write your room number on my hand? I sleepwalk at night and I'd rather not walk into the lobby butt naked one more time.

Quick warning before this plane takes off: I'm not a good flyer. So if I start to freak out, I'm going to need you to calm me down.

I have one of those "whatever happens on the road, stays on the road" policies. Get used to it.

**Atlanta**: This is where Coke is headquartered.

**Baltimore**: Didn't you just love *The Wire*? Omar comin'!

**Boston**: I've been practicing my Boston accent. We're gonna blend right in.

**Chicago**: Is this the "Show Me City" or is that another thing?

**Dallas**: How 'bout them Cowboys?

**Los Angeles**: Do you know where the girls from *The Hills* hang out?

**Miami**: I hope we run into Crockett and Tubbs.

**New York**: It actually used to be called New Amsterdam.

**Orlando**: Wanna just blow off the meetings and hit Disney World?

**San Francisco**: Before we get there, we should probably practice hating Los Angeles.

**Seattle**: Did you know this is where they invented coffee?

**St. Louis**: I'm not leaving till I get a look at that arch.

# AFTER A FIGHT WITH A COWORKER

Are you and I...OK?

I hope we never fight ever again about anything ever.

From now on, let's just smush our feelings deep down inside ourselves. It worked for my parents.

I think we should see a therapist together.

For a minute there I thought we were going to swing.

You're still my dawg, dawg.

I promise you, this will only make our relationship stronger.

Let's head to the paintball field and put this whole thing behind us the old-fashioned way.

Hold me.

You lucky S.O.B.

You did that on purpose, right?

Pain is temporary. Disability checks are forever.

Giant settlement, here you come.

I know a very shady doctor who will be more than happy to testify on your behalf.

Assuming this injury will heal but still give you cover to claim that you suffer chronic pain, this is truly the greatest day of your life.

You should call a TV lawyer and sue the pants off everyone.

You gotta play through the pain.

Rub some dirt on it.

I hope you took the advice of that duck and got Aflac.

There goes our accident-free workplace initiative. Now we don't get a pizza lunch.

# "WANNA WORK ON THIS TOGETHER?"

First, tell me your vision.

Tell me one thing: can I trust you with my life?

I'm honored just to be asked.

You start and I'll join you when you're mostly done.

I do, but I'm contractually forbidden.

Like as a team?

Hmmm...I'm guessing that would involve us talking.

Would we have to be in the same room for that or could we do it via email?

Depends on how much you already have done.

Sure. Then afterwards, let's get an apartment together.

Did someone say we had to? Otherwise, not at all.

Not really. I kind of want to keep my job.

No. Unless I'll get fired if I don't. Then I totally do.

If you're willing to do 80 percent of it, I'm in.

OK, but I'm hogging all the credit.

# TO A COWORKER WHO WANTS TO START A UNION

Look at Norma Rae over here.

Stick it to the man.

I'm worried about management bringing in goons.

I'm in, but only if we get the Mob involved.

I don't know, I always kind of wanted to be a scab.

Management says that unions haven't ever done anything worthwhile.

Hey—I'll be honest—I'm in this for me and me only.

Let's start a softball league first, move on to a book club and then see where that takes us.

And how exactly would forming some kind of massive, collective bargaining unit that stands up for all of our interests together benefit me?

The only union I want to join is the Union of the Snake. Where my Duran Duran fans at?

Only if it means I can call in sick whenever I want and my boss can't do crap about it.

I'm sure the market will sort it out.

# WHILE ON STRIKE

I'm starting to understand why the French like this so much.

Who brought the lawn chairs?

No justice! No peace! No justice! No peace! Just kidding, we just want our dental plan.

Why do we have to walk in circles? Can't we just sit in our lawn chairs and convey the same sense of purpose?

Being out here sure beats being stuck inside doing jobs we all hate anyway.

We should add in some crazy demands like free packing tape and hugs every morning when we get to work.

What are you guys gonna do if the riot police start shooting tear gas?

Anyone see any goons?

I hope some goons show up soon.

I could really get into being on the news being attacked by goons.

Let's go kick some scab butt.

I'm all out of clever chant ideas.

# AT A TEAM-BUILDING RETREAT

Who's ready to trust-fall?

This better not turn into some *Lord of the Flies*–type situation.

I'm already starting to feel guilty for selling those trade secrets to our competitors.

I hope we get a souvenir T-shirt that I can wear to company softball games next year.

So...do you think there's a trust-fall?

I come for the team building, but I stay for the trust-falls.

There better be trust-falling or I'm totally out of here.

I just hope I don't have to catch Ned during the trust-fall. That guy's a bull moose.

Trust-falls are actually how Anthony Robbins got his start.

I wonder who will be the first one voted off the island.

And whoever survives the longest in the woods without food or water wins a million dollars. I wish they had these more often. I'd probably work a lot harder.

I'll be happy when this is over and I can get back to doing real work.

Suffice it to say, I just found out that I'm a massive lawsuit waiting to happen.

I think I need a shower.

Huh. That was illuminating.

Well, everyone, I am Super Gluing my mouth shut. Been nice talking with you.

During that seminar, did anyone else keep thinking, "Uh-oh"?

I hope I'm not the only one who feels dirty now.

I'm scared to look at or talk to any of my coworkers now.

I'm gonna play things safe and just sexually harass strangers at the supermarket.

Do you think the attorney who taught the seminar would go out with me?

They were kidding about all that stuff, right?

Fine. But how am I supposed to get dates if I can't aggressively target coworkers?

# IF YOU DON'T WANT TO GET SUED FOR SEXUAL HARASSMENT

Hi. (Keep walking and keep eyes above coworker's forehead.)

# BEFORE AN UNEXPECTED AND MYSTERIOUS COMPANY MEETING

Why do I get the feeling we're about to get Rick Rolled?

Just in case, keep the exits clear.

I think it was Professor Plum with the candlestick holder.

Whiskey Tango Foxtrot is this all about?

Who are we missing?

If we're all in here, then who's running the company?

I hope this isn't about all the paper clips I've stolen.

Raise your hand if you think you're about to get fired.

We should all get together like this more often.

Surprise!

It's quiet in here. Almost too quiet.

I heard that the boss wants us to reinvent the wheel.

I bet the company was finally bought by a Dubai equity fund.

I feel like I'm going to throw up.

# MEANINGLESS ANSWERS TO COWORKERS' QUESTIONS

## "HOW WAS YOUR QUARTER?"

Somewhere between huge and colossal.

They will write epic poems about it some day.

We threaded the needle.

Let's just say, there's pretty much no stopping us now.

Now that the bribes are flowing freely, we're really starting to pick up steam.

Whatever a synonym for amazing is, that's your answer.

My quarter was more like a dollar.

Let's just say my next lease won't be a mid-size sedan.

Well, let's just put it this way: terrible.

After the quarter I just had, my next goal is to keep from being asked to leave the company.

It was so good I feel like Knight Rider.

My back hurts from all the bags of money I'm dragging in here.

Midas-esque.

# WHEN THEY BRING IN AN OUTSIDE CONSULTANT

I fear change.

Consult, from the Latin, meaning "to fire."

Any of you talk with him and you're all dead to me.

Time to start reviewing our best practices.

Maybe this will help us move forward on our virtual community.

Now we'll finally get some creative decision making.

Time to break out the group think.

I hope this helps us to create a learning organization that can adapt quickly.

I hope we get a little more lean 'n' mean.

We definitely could use some pointers on how we can be a nimbler organization.

I've been waiting to hear some ideas for how we can reduce our carbon footprint.

If you just keep saying, "Quality is free," you should be all right.

This is like a reality show and they get to eliminate us one at a time.

Does this mean we have to fight them?

They can take our company, but they'll never take my stapler!

I hope it's a Japanese company. I hear they have very progressive and employee-friendly policies.

Block the doors!

Wow. This means people think we're doing something right.

They'll never take us alive! Who's with me?

I hope this means buyout offers.

Gentlemen, start your shredders.

Awesome. We're going to be on CNBC.

If we turn ourselves in now, we may avoid hard time.

Them coppers ain't takin' me alive.

He's not going to do well inside. His skin is like butter.

Even money he flees to Argentina.

Bring the truck around. We need to steal us some office supplies.

Great. Another one of my bosses indicted by the SEC. That's four for four.

I didn't rat him out.

I shotgun his office!

That would explain the garbage bags filled with cash.

Now I'll never have a chance to drive his Porsche.

They haven't yet built a prison that could hold him.

Do you think we'll get to testify against him?

I hope I can make my mortgage payment.

Do you know anyone who is looking to buy a like-new mansion? Or maybe 100,000 delinquent subprime mortgages?

In retrospect, the whole "Masters of the Universe" thing might have been a bit much.

If only we could pay our short-term debt obligations with hubris. We'd be more than covered.

Let me know if you hear of anyone interested in buying a used car.

Can you remind me why none of us saw this coming?

I hope I don't run into anyone from Main Street on the way out to my car.

Napoleon said, "In victory, you deserve champagne; in defeat, you need it." Now I wish I hadn't used all my champagne to wash my Ferrari.

I'm going to head to my place in the south of France until this whole thing blows over.

I hate to say it, but I told you all this was going to happen.

# WHEN YOUR CORPORATION GETS A GOVERNMENT BAILOUT

I knew remembering the Treasury Secretary's birthday every year would eventually pay off!

I always knew we were too important to fail!

Sweet. Now we can still be sure that all the executives get massive bonuses.

Is there any way some of that money can go into getting the office fridge cleaned?

Are they going to send us some government cheese too?

Guess I can't rant about the downfall of Enron anymore.

It's like our whole company is on unemployment.

We better not blow it again.

Let's put it all on red, double or nothing.

I almost feel guilty. Almost.

# WHEN THE ECONOMY COLLAPSES

If you think about it, this might be a really good time to buy stock.

I bet we can make the Great Depression not look so great.

Just last week I was saying this could happen.

It's gonna be boom times for alcohol, tobacco and firearms, as well as the agency that controls them.

I'm glad I was so bullish on Smith & Wesson.

I'll trade you ten shares of Google stock for some canned tuna.

I sure will miss satellite TV and running water.

Any day now they're gonna start paying us with bullets and bread.

Would it be OK if my entire family moved into your basement?

I love those shoes you're wearing. They'd make a great stew.

From now on the employee of the month gets a can of tomato soup.

# POWER PHRASES

## NOW THAT'S WHAT I CALL ____.

Now that's what I call a tire rotation.

Now that's what I call an insurance estimate.

Now that's what I call a color copy.

Now that's what I call an iced caramel latte.

Now that's what I call a catheter change.

Now that's what I call underwriting.

Now that's what I call Lasik surgery.

Now that's what I call a dovetail joint.

Now that's what I call aerating a lawn.

Now that's what I call a rental agreement.

# CHAPTER 6
# OFFICE POLITICS

Run away while there's still time!

You must really hate yourself.

I'll give you my job if you really want it.

So you think you're going to replace me, do you? Good luck.

Don't worry. It gets easier after the first four rounds.

Quick heads up: the boss loves profanity, so swear up a storm during the interview.

I remember what it was like to be you. Hope is a cruel thing.

So you decided to give up on playing centerfield for the Yankees?

Don't look at the boss' left eye. It's made out of glass.

Did you make a wrong turn or something?

Seems like you're fitting in.

They say the first day is the hardest.

Pop quiz: what's my name?

It's all downhill from here.

Remember everyone's name yet?

You know, the guy you replaced was a very close friend of mine.

The guy you replaced, we used to hunt together on the weekends.

I'm impressed. The last guy didn't make it to lunch.

Are you ready for the hazing rituals?

Kind of feels like the first day of school, doesn't it?

I'm sorry, but I'm going to have to ask for your lunch money.

Just so you know how big a deal this is, we interviewed literally tens of thousands of other applicants for this job.

We hired a guy who looks just like you.

We gotta get you a nickname. How do you feel about "Dawg"?

I have a feeling you and I are going to be very, very close friends.

The guy you're replacing disappeared under mysterious circumstances, so just be careful.

Still here?

Only two months and twenty-nine days till those benefits kick in.

I don't want to get too close to you until we know if you're gonna get fired or not.

Tell me your last name so I can look you up on Facebook.

Here's something to remember around here: if you're gonna come at the king, you best not miss.

The first thing is to figure out where the restrooms are.

You got the hang of it yet?

I bet you got this down cold already, right?

I look forward to your transferring calls to my desk.

If anyone calls for a Generalissimo Fernando, that's me.

You know, this is how Warren Buffett got his start.

You don't have to worry about me, I'm not the harassing type.

If a monkey in a butler's outfit comes in looking lost, give me a ring.

Does the phone usually ring when somebody calls?

What's the worst thing that's happened so far?

I'm sure you're doing your share of eavesdropping.

Are you enjoying the free Internet?

Meet me in the parking lot at midnight. This place isn't what it seems.

Do you prefer secretary, receptionist or executive assistant?

I love what you've done with the place.

If anyone gives you a hard time, you come to me.

Are you having fun yet?

Did you memorize everyone's extension?

Don't ever forget: you are our first line of defense against annoying phone calls.

Where can I park my horse?

Don't worry, this place isn't a *Mad Men*–type situation.

# "WHAT DO YOU MAKE OF THE NEW BOSS?"

Likable enough, but it's still a boss.

I'm still getting a read on things.

I love the new boss. Hey, are you a spy or something?

I think whatever the company tells me to think.

Why, did you hear something?

I've seen worse.

A+ call by management.

Like I'm supposed to believe you're not wearing a wire.

I'm going to reserve judgment until I see him around the female interns at the next going-away party.

So far he seems more Tony Soprano than whoever the TV version of a really cool, awesome boss is.

I like her, but I think we got off on the wrong foot when I asked if I could call her "Mom."

Time will probably tell.

# TO A NEW TRANSFER
# FROM ANOTHER OFFICE

I heard that your old office was a front for the CIA.

We do things a little differently around here.

Welcome to the majors, kid!

You ain't a spy, is you?

You're like a long lost relative.

It's almost like you got switched at birth at the hospital and all these years later, boom, here you are.

We had to give up a first-round draft pick and a worker to be named later to get you here.

We welcome new people to our office by having them tell us all the most embarrassing thing that's ever happened to them.

Just in case you heard otherwise, we work hard and we play hard.

Your hazing begins tomorrow at 5 a.m. Be in the parking lot and don't wear any metal.

Is it true that your old office was filled with vampires?

If you find out that our branch is working too hard, please let me know.

# TO THE EMPLOYEE
# OF THE MONTH

Your college degree just paid for itself.

I imagine this makes you one of the top candidates for
Employee of the Year.

The wife must be going nuts.

How are you going to spend your winnings?

This means that the next four weeks are all about you.

This isn't going to change our relationship, is it?

Can I touch your plaque?

Give me a hint. How'd you do it?

It's all downhill from here.

Can you put in a good word for me with the boss?

I always knew you had it in you.

I hope you use your position to raise awareness about pet
overpopulation.

Slow down, Turbo—you're making the rest of us look bad.

Does this mean you're too good for me now?

And here I thought all of your sucking up was a complete waste of time.

Well I guess that proves to the rest of us that anyone here can get a raise.

Who's buying drinks…and steak…and a new Blue Ray player for me?

Are you going to start dressing better now?

That's what you get when you use "The Secret."

You should have asked for a corner office.

Now aren't you glad you decided to skip grad school?

I don't care about things like raises. I measure my work by lives changed. And that, dear friends, is why I sell vinyl siding.

Hello V6 engine and leather seats.

Don't let this change you, Pony Boy. Or stay gold or something.

It's less a corporate ladder and more like an elevator for you.

Might be time for you to incorporate.

I hope you have a will drafted.

Congratulations and welcome to the next tax bracket.

I'd like to believe you worked hard and earned it.

The first thing you should do is buy a yacht.

I knew you had it in you.

You make it look so easy.

Can I borrow your smoke and mirrors?

Someone just won the work lottery.

Hey there, Miss Overachiever.

I wish I had your kind of commitment to this dead-end job.

Guess you're going to find out if money can buy happiness.

Oprah is proud of you.

There's always next time.

I guess they didn't show you the money.

They can't put a price on your family's love.

You could start buying groceries at the dollar store.

It seems many of us know your actual value to the company.

Since you didn't get that raise, coffee is on me. Meet me at the coffee machine in five minutes.

I guess you'll have to make it up by selling stolen office supplies on eBay.

Well maybe the country will go through an unprecedented period of deflation which will make your current salary incrementally more powerful.

Who needs money? You can't use it to buy anything anyway.

You'll get the next one.

There is no justice.

I'm sorry, but that's total BS.

Listen, if you had that job, they'd own you.

He must be a Freemason.

I hear he made one of those "Indecent Proposal" deals with the boss.

Sure, but do you know how much overtime she's going to have to work?

Rome wasn't built in a day.

I'm going to talk to HR. She used "The Secret," and that can't be legal.

If you had gotten that job, you and I couldn't have hung out anymore anyway.

You didn't want that promotion. All it meant was more money and a better title.

I knew I should have paid closer attention in Sucking Up 101 during freshman year of college.

You need to set your goals lower next time.

We need to start failing upward too.

Now this is what we call a morale builder.

I hear his father just bought the company.

Just what this company needs: more management.

At least we got a nice reminder that merit and talent really don't matter here.

I kind of like the way my insides taste.

You know how they say every cloud has a silver lining? Let's keep telling ourselves that.

Sure he's totally fake and steals ideas from people and tells management lies about the rest of us, but I'm sure it wasn't that.

Yet again, education and experience have shown themselves to be wildly overrated.

Maybe he was due some karma from a past life.

## MEANINGLESS ANSWERS TO COWORKERS' QUESTIONS

# "DO YOU LIKE WORKING HERE?"

It's like summer camp.

It's the best job I love to hate.

I wouldn't say I don't like it.

Never felt more fulfilled.

It's the best job I've had this week.

It would be better if they upgraded the candy machine.

The pay's terrible, but what's important is that I'm making a difference.

Before I got this job I was living in a tent city down by the rail yard. So yeah, this is pretty cool.

I get to spend eight to ten hours a day with my coworkers. What do you think?

I need to jackhammer the smile off my face at the end of the day.

Like a fat kid likes cake.

No, but I do enjoy money, which I use to buy food and pay rent, so that's good.

Not as much as I like the company discount.

I would, but I honestly have no idea who the hell you are.

Sure. But first drop and give me twenty.

Just write whatever and forge my signature.

I recommend you pick me up a bottle of Scotch.

For you, anything.

If I do, will you finally make me a friend on Facebook?

I have a better idea. How about I write a song about your talents?

In return I'd like you to write a composition about what you like about me.

This place won't be the same without you.

Going, going, gone.

Let me get one last good look at you so I can remember you just like this.

Don't you forget about me.

Promise me you'll keep in touch.

Please don't look at me, because I'm this close to bawling.

I knew we'd never be able to keep someone as capable as you.

We really are going to miss you, until you start coming by to visit regularly at which point we'll find you a little annoying.

See you around the bend.

I guess you're an uncaged bird now, and if you don't come back, then you were never really ours to begin with.

Run and don't ever look back.

So you finally escaped, huh?

# WHEN A COWORKER SUDDENLY QUITS IN A HUFF

He seemed upset.

Probably just needs to cool off.

That was interesting.

Did you know that the Chinese word for "quitting suddenly" is the same as the word for "opportunity"?

Can you still file for unemployment when you scream at everyone?

So does this mean we're not getting two-weeks' notice?

I wonder if he's still coming on the retreat.

I wonder what the silver lining here is.

Dibs on his parking spot!

For how much longer does he still get his employee discount?

I just hope he stole a cup of coffee on the way out.

At least he can sleep in tomorrow. There's that.

I thought I saw him working on his resumé.

# TO A COWORKER WHO JUST GOT LAID OFF

Our loss is your couch's gain.

Now you can finish that novel you've been putting off.

Who needs a job anyway? Unless, I mean, you don't have a trust fund like I do.

You had to know this was going to happen. The rest of us knew about three months ago.

If you need to borrow some money, don't hesitate to ask your parents.

Can I have your parking spot?

Well we do have some great memories. Like that time we...er... well it was great working with you.

Boy, am I jealous. I really am. I guess I'll just have to comfort myself with the money and dental benefits this job provides.

Boom. Outta here.

I'd stand up for you, but if they fired me I'd be devastated.

At least you have your woodworking skills to fall back on.

Can I help you with your resumé?

Look at this not as an end, but as a new beginning.

# TO A COWORKER WHO JUST GOT LAID OFF

Don't think of it as a door closing. Think of it as a door smacking you in the face.

Hey, you'll always have a place to stay in my garage.

If it were up to me, I would have given you one more chance.

Who's the bread winner now?

Look on the bright side—you don't have to pay any taxes.

Maybe you'll hit the lottery.

Now you can take that vacation you've always talked about.

This is the best thing that could have ever happened to you. I'm not sure why or how, but you'll find out eventually.

Can I have your leftovers in the fridge?

Try to remember that one person's negative is another person's positive.

And what's even worse is that Phil is actually the one who committed gross misconduct.

They'll never take us alive.

I assume you're fine with me not going down with you.

Well, you had a good run.

If it makes you feel better I'll stand on my desk and call you "My Captain" when they haul you out of here.

Can I have your chair?

Don't worry. We'll be OK without you.

Settle down. Now let's figure out how this is going to help both of our careers.

Maybe they'll give me your office, though.

I'll miss you.

## MEANINGLESS ANSWERS TO COWORKERS' QUESTIONS

# "WHERE DO YOU SEE YOURSELF IN FIVE YEARS?"

Hopefully napping.

Hanging out, doing stuff.

Seriously, what does that even mean?

Doing "edgy" comedy.

Adding Facebook friends.

Being a billionaire, at the very least.

I figure I'll be on TV promoting a line of workout DVDs.

Older, wiser and less fertile.

In some professional sports hall of fame.

Big pimpin'.

Probably on a post Olympics victory tour.

In a bomb shelter in northern Idaho.

President. Of America.

Hopefully opening a new branch of this company on Mars.

# WHEN A FIRED EMPLOYEE IS BEING ESCORTED FROM THE BUILDING

Good thing they're escorting him out and making sure he forgets where the office is so he can't come back later.

I hope they grabbed his ID badge.

Good thing the paparazzi aren't around for this.

They're not gonna kill him, are they?

I guess he just knows too much.

I hope they're armed. His whole body is a deadly weapon.

I have a feeling he's gonna land on his head before he lands on his feet.

I got a feeling his exit interview will include a little waterboarding.

Looks like the company softball team needs a new shortstop.

I had no idea he was so scrappy. That's the kind of fighter we want on our side.

That went well.

# WHEN YOU BUMP INTO A FORMER COWORKER WHO WAS FIRED

Hi. (Keep walking.)

I was just thinking about you the other day.

Life is too short to reminisce.

What are you up to these days?

Dude, you got out of there at exactly the right time.

You're not missing much, believe me.

I'm actually kind of jealous of you.

You look great—and so much happier.

The whole place is going downhill fast.

Oh, I really like your shoes. Where did you get those?

I got a doctor's appointment I gotta get to.

Hey, great seeing you!

Now's when life really begins, right?

Now, you can tell me, are you retiring or getting forced out?

The last twenty years must have just flown by.

Thanks for the memories.

Anyone you want to insult before you go?

You'll still come around, right?

Now you can do everything on your Bucket List.

Any travel plans?

*Hasta la vista*, baby.

Don't worry, Social Security won't run out for a good ten years. Twelve years tops.

Time to start practicing for the Senior Golf Tour.

Take me with you.

I've been meaning to tell you this for years, my name isn't (your name), it's actually Robin.

Any nostalgia?

# WHEN YOU START A NEW JOB

I'm just so excited to be here.

Hope you guys can show me the ropes.

I can't believe these people hired me.

I'm ready for a vacation.

Help me out...what exactly is my job again?

Who has thumbs and is the new guy? RIGHT HERE! (Point to yourself with your thumbs.)

Let's hope this doesn't end with me getting escorted out of the building again.

So, who in this place knows how to party?

I'm terrible with names, so if everyone could wear name tags, that'd be great.

I have a feeling like we're all gonna end up being best friends forever.

So, any office gossip I need to know?

# WHEN YOU GET YOUR COMPANY ID BADGE

Now show me the secret handshake!

I guess it's official now.

Does this get me into the executive washroom?

And where do I leave the blood sample?

So this thing allows you guys to track me wherever I go?

This picture makes me look fat, but with a "ph"!

Can you take my picture again? I look like a criminal in this.

It was only a matter of time.

The answer is that yes, sucking up to me works.

I can't wait to tell my college sweetheart about this.

Payback time!

I guess I'll have to upgrade the old Taurus now.

Don't worry, I'm the same old (your name) I was yesterday.

Now we can make all those changes we've talked about.

Sure, the money's nice and so is the title and so is the recognition and the added power and the bigger office—but what's really important to me is that I did it through good old-fashioned work ethic.

Not gonna lie to you guys—being recognized as the best is a good feeling.

Guess who's gonna make this year's "Who's Who in America?"

Now what do I do?

## MEANINGLESS ANSWERS TO COWORKERS' QUESTIONS

## "WHAT KIND OF MOOD IS THE BOSS IN TODAY?"

He's like a ray of sunshine on a cloudy day.

I'd wear a bomb-squad suit if I were you.

Be on the lookout for flying staplers.

Warm and cuddly.

He specifically said today's a good day to ask for a raise. You should get in there.

Looks like he spent the night in a cave with armadillos.

Ornery with a chance of tantrums.

I think the stress is starting to make her regret stabbing all of us in the back to get ahead.

She's as fake and transparently climb-y as ever.

There's only one way to find out, and that is to throw hot coffee in his face.

Like a wolverine going through nicotine withdrawal.

The only way to know for sure is to screw up.

If you've got any ideas, he's looking to steal a few.

# WHEN YOUR DEPARTMENT IS MAKING CUTBACKS

I wonder how many pens I can fit in my briefcase?

Salary, smalary. I pay myself in free coffee and paper clips.

If they fire me it's straight to the PGA Tour.

Dead man walking.

Those fat cats upstairs have no idea what it's like for us down here in the trenches.

I haven't seen this many pink slips since the Victoria's Secret catalog.

If either of us gets fired, the other one should quit in protest.

We should be fine, but I hear the Akron office is screwed.

I know how we can save the company some money: coupons.

Good luck getting rid of me. I'm like a cockroach. I'll always be here when the lights are off.

Is this an office or a zombie movie?

# WHEN YOU GET FIRED

So...this is kind of awkward.

I should have seen this coming.

I'm not gonna lie to you—this really gums up my weekend plans.

I'll be back. But I don't mean that in a crazy-former-employee way. I just mean to say "hi" sometime. Unless security bans me from the building, which I would totally understand.

And now I get led away in handcuffs?

Are we still on for beers later?

This means I'm no longer on the company softball team?

Can I walk out, come back, quit, and we can pretend like you never fired me?

You'll come crawling back. They always do.

You can't fire me. I stopped working here months ago.

I'm going to give you a moment to think before you make the biggest mistake of your life.

I'll just take my letter of recommendation and be on my way.

Let's all keep in touch.

Don't worry, I'll be around.

I've learned a lot from everyone here.

This is the best group of people I've ever worked with.

None of you will ever be far from my thoughts and fears.

I'll always have a special place for each of you in my heart.

I'll miss you the most of all, Scarecrow.

I never thought this day would come.

Well, I was planning to take my last day at the job to tell you all what I actually think of you, but instead I think I'll just say it was nice working with you.

See ya later, suckers.

I guess now's as good a time as any to tell all of you that I never actually did anything here.

Look me up on Facebook.

# POWER PHRASES

## IT'S ____ PALOOZA IN HERE.

It's Bankpalooza in here.

It's X-raypalooza in here.

It's Shippingandreceivingpalooza in here.

It's Butcherpalooza in here.

It's Haberdasherypalooza in here.

It's Dividendreinvestmentpalooza in here.

It's Industrialchemistrypalooza in here.

It's Wallpaperpalooza in here.

It's Alterationpalooza in here.

It's Pedicurepalooza in here.

It's Telemarketpalooza in here.

It's Espressopalooza in here.

## CHAPTER 7
# NOT YOUR EVERYDAY BANTER

Or at least that's the word on the street.

That's the buzz.

Or so people are saying.

And that's what is the what.

That's the stick in the honey.

Don't quote me on that.

Careful: loose lips sink ships.

Remember: knowledge is power.

Sorry if I just shocked your mind.

You didn't hear it from me.

Be very careful what you do with this.

Something like this was inevitable.

But don't freak out here.

What can you do.

Omar comin'!

Give it to me. I can handle the truth.

Whoa, I'm not going to hurt you.

Someone's hiding something.

Next time I'll wear my wooden shoes so you can hear me coming.

Do you care to share with the rest of the class?

You're both going on my "list."

I studied for years to be a ninja, which is how I was able to sneak up on you like this.

Words hurt. Not as much as sharp sticks, but they do hurt.

I'm going to assume you were talking about how wonderful it is to work with me.

How would you like it if you caught me during one of the many times throughout the day that I talk badly about you?

Twenty bucks would go a long way to making me feel better.

I got a memo saying I should come see you two about something important.

Huh.

# WHEN SOMEONE'S OFFICE CHAIR BREAKS

I have Super Glue.

Time to check out the salad bar.

Think you can fix it?

I guess it lost its will to live.

It's all right—they were already interviewing replacement chairs.

Funny, that's the exact snapping sound a Workers' Comp claim makes.

What'd you do to it?

Good luck explaining this one.

You should write about this on your blog.

Go straight to a foreign doctor and get a cast. Then you can sue and get a big settlement.

You all right, dude?

# TO A COWORKER RUNNING THROUGH THE OFFICE

Women and children first!

You look really dedicated to your job right now!

Who's chasing you?

You can run, but you can't hide!

Gangway!

Getting ready for the Olympics?

Run, you'll get there faster.

Go, go, go!

Did someone move your cheese?

Where's the fire?

Clear!

You can't run forever!

## "HAVE YOU TRIED OUT THAT NEW SPA?"

I would, but the thing is I don't like relaxing.

I find spas spooky and weird.

No, but I already have scented candles at home.

I don't even know what you're talking about.

You mean that place is legit? I thought it was a front for human trafficking.

No, but I'm glad to know you're concerned with my spa habits.

I haven't been inside, but it gives off really good energy.

I'm very confident that you and I should never go there together.

No, but when I do, you'll be the first person I tell.

Every weekend for the past month.

Now's the part where you want us to go to a spa day together.

You kidding me? That place keeps me sane.

Good evening.

How do you do?

Welcome, friend.

Give me like three minutes and it's all yours.

I'm here to help you.

Cool it, Senator Craig.

I never knew that that was how you felt.

You got me!

Please, don't be embarrassed. Many people don't consider other people either.

Hold on, I'll scoot over.

At least buy me a drink first.

# WHEN A COWORKER LEAVES THE KITCHEN A MESS

It's really a mess in here.

Looks like a food hurricane made landfall.

Did I miss a food fight?

This checks out.

And...my appetite is gone.

Did we get a pet bear that I don't know about?

Smart of Hansel to leave a trail of breadcrumbs back to his desk.

We have gotta stop putting broccoli in the microwave.

Can I lick the bowl?

I wish people would treat the office kitchen like they would their own kitchen.

Ahhhh, a dirty office kitchen...no surer sign that we've all collectively chucked it in.

Was someone making paella?

It's like the inside of Jabba the Hutt in here.

Yup.

Just like old times.

They should really put a padlock on this thing.

Maybe I'm not hungry.

If we just had some bay leaves we could whip up some *coq au vin*.

Can I roundhouse kick an apple off your head?

Who stole my lunch?

The amount of peanuts I can eat is truly astonishing.

We gotta start stocking liquor.

I wonder what will require the least amount of flossing.

I chew my food one hundred times before swallowing.

I'd bet that I know more things about pudding than anyone else here.

I like these events that remind us how little it takes to satisfy us.

This is so much better than money.

Is this considered taxable income?

Chomp.

Saturated fats make me forgetful.

For free pizza, I'd follow the boss to the very gates of hell.

# WHEN SOMEONE WANTS TO TALK POLITICS

I don't read newspapers.

I just think they're all crooks.

I vote for whoever is first on the ballot.

I really don't have time to keep up with that stuff. I'm way too busy focusing on my work.

Did you see Obama's Hawaii vacation pics? He's more ripped than that Bowflex guy.

We shouldn't talk about this unless we schedule an official debate.

I don't know anything about these local elections. I'm registered in Alaska so I can mail in an absentee ballot for Sarah Palin.

I just write in my mom. She's the only person I trust to do what's right for the children.

Look, I voted for Obama, so I don't need to vote because I already *did* my part to save the world.

We don't really need a third party so much as we need a *second* party. Am I right? (Offer high-five.)

# TO THE GUY WHO REALLY WANTS TO BE YOUR FRIEND

I'll totally give you a ring this weekend if my parents' flight gets canceled.

I'm still getting over this flu.

What if we become friends and you realize that you hate me?

We can't hang out. I just can't get hurt again.

No can do. My BFF is a psycho who'll hurt you bad.

I've been looking for a kidney donor for years, let's go get blood tests this weekend!

I didn't want to tell anyone, but I'm a vampire, so you can see how this won't work out.

Sorry, no time for anyone else. I'm p-whipped.

My parole office will need to run a background check on you before we do any hanging out.

I'm flattered but...is my office phone ringing?

So do you love heroin, Indian food and Celine Dion too?

Just so you know, I hate crowds and I cry a lot. If you can handle that, you're in. Oh, and I borrow a lot of money.

Let's try Facebook first and see where it goes.

Looking good, gotta go.

Can't talk, contagious.

Gotta run, my eBay auction ends in 30 seconds.

Sorry, I heard my car's being towed!

Sorry, but there are some CDC guys in hazmat suits at reception who really want to talk to me.

Gotta run. HR says I need to use a vacation day from 2001 today or I'll lose it forever.

You don't want to be between me and the bathroom right now.

My dad just called me from his death bed and apparently he has some pretty big news for me. Something about a brother I have in Sao Paolo.

Must get insulin!

Bees! (While running and swatting.)

Have you seen the fire marshall?

Remind me later on to tell you why I'm so busy right now.

BRB.

# WHEN THE BUILDING'S FIRE ALARM GOES OFF

Who burned the popcorn this time?

Sure do hope that this wasn't from the cigarette I snuck in the supply room.

Out of my way, people!

If we back out of here slowly, we can be at Chili's in ten minutes.

If only this bad boy were burning for real we'd finally be free.

I always dreamed of being a fireman. There's nothing I cherish more than saving human lives.

I like watching the fire department act like they're taking this seriously.

Save yourselves. It's too late for me.

In the event of an actual fire, fear can save your life. Think about that.

Do I need to practice stopping, dropping and rolling?

I have to go back inside. I need to save my expense reports.

So in a real emergency am I still supposed to play Tetris on my phone until help arrives?

# "DO YOU KNOW A GOOD PLACE TO BUY SUCH-AND-SUCH?"

I do all my shopping by catalog.

I just bought one and got the best deal ever, but that deal is over so you can't get it for that price.

Meet me in the alley after work. Bring cash.

You know, Wal-Mart is open 24 hours a day.

Have you checked the liquor store? That's where I buy a lot of things.

I don't buy anything anymore. Everything breaks.

Unless it's drugs, I'm not the guy to ask.

I think answering that question would mean somehow crossing a work life–personal life boundary.

No, but I know where to buy an illegal handgun.

My personal shopper gets everything for me.

I can make you one in my workshop. I'm handy.

It's not an issue of finding a good place to buy it, it's an issue of finding the right place to buy it.

Hello, Smarty. It's called eBay!

Who left the window open?

Think I can get a day off out of this?

The interns get weirder and weirder every year.

Careful. I saw on Discovery Channel that they can be quite dangerous.

I told management this would happen, but no one listened.

I wish I had paid more attention during the sexual-harassment/ wild-animal workshop.

Remember: he's way more scared of us than we are of him.

Do we have a wild-animal insurance policy?

How is this different from any other day in this place?

On the one day I forget my 30-30.

Do you know how much jerky we could make if we caught it?

For earthquakes you get under the desk, for wild animals you stand still. Right?

When I wanted to buy a tranquilizer gun for the office, everyone laughed. But who's laughing now? The cougar in the conference room, that's who.

I can't wait to write about this in my blog.

No reason to wait to call the carpet cleaner.

Can I pet it?

That's it. I don't care what time it is. I'm starting happy hour right now.

Quiet please. I'm playing solitaire over here.

Why couldn't it have been a monkey?

I'm not shoveling that up.

Is this one of those singing telegrams?

Now who's encroaching on whose natural habitat?

This really may be the best day of my life.

I better be getting time and a half for this.

Someone start singing. They say that music soothes even the most savage beast.

Give it a cubicle and put it to work.

Doesn't it realize I have deadlines?

# WHEN YOUR OFFICE HAS BEEN DESTROYED IN A NATURAL DISASTER

That was weird.

I'm just glad the boss is OK.

I hope they remembered to get insurance.

Anyone wanna try to make happy hour?

And I was almost entirely caught up on my expense reports.

Just when we had the office decorated the way we wanted.

In what way could this turn out to somehow be my fault?

I hope this doesn't jeopardize the company picnic.

I wonder what happened to my stapler.

Are we still gonna get paid for showing up to work today?

And I left my nonreimbursed expense report receipts in there.

This is why I was pushing so hard for all of us to work from home.

We can rebuild and make it almost as good as it was before.

Anyone have anything trite to say?

## TO YOUR COWORKER IF YOUR ERROR
## JUST CAUSED A NUCLEAR MELTDOWN

Well, I guess we can *glow* home now.

I have a feeling this is going to take a lot of paperwork to straighten out.

Well, there goes employee of the month for me.

Boy, oh boy, am I glad I rent.

This is a great example of why we need to invest heavily in solar power.

I think we're going to be on the news.

That will leave a mark.

Do you think anyone will notice?

We'd better think of a good excuse.

Oy vey.

Mama said there'd be days like this.

**POWER PHRASES**

## _____ OR BUST!

A raise or bust!

Compression-molded-plastics convention or bust!

Ten percent over third quarter projections or bust!

Corner office or bust!

Copies or bust!

Short nap in my car or bust!

Let me drive this school bus or bust!

Balanced books or bust!

Uncover this rogue regime's nuclear program or bust!

# CHAPTER 8
# SICK DAYS, HOLIDAYS, WEEKENDS AND OTHER DAYS TOO

I hope it's OK; I don't want to let the team down.

I would feel terrible if I got anyone else sick.

Am I coughing enough, or should I ramp it up?

My doctor said I'm definitely contagious.

I don't remember the exact diagnosis but I heard "bird" and "Taiwan."

The thermometer literally melted in my mouth. Literally.

I'll come in later if I feel better.

I may not make it through the day.

The next 24 hours—if I survive—will be the most painful in my life.

Don't make a big deal please. Don't send flowers or anything.

I'd come in, but the CDC has sealed me inside my home.

If you love the sound of hacking mucus, I'm your guy.

Don't worry. With what you guys pay me, I can't afford to call in sick and go to the ball game.

# TO A COWORKER WHO COMES TO WORK SICK

Here you are at work, even though you're going to make all of us sick too. Talk about dedication to craft!

It's like that movie *Outbreak*, only without Morgan Freeman and popcorn.

So the CDC said your strain of the flu isn't contagious?

Let me know what medicine is keeping you going so next week I'll know what to take.

The only acceptable reason for you to come in is if your cable is out.

Who are you, Castro?

Did you get a chance to touch my keyboard and mouse yet?

So when I get what you have should I come to work too?

This is great, I've always wanted to be quarantined.

For the sake of convenience, just sneeze directly into my mouth.

Hey Captain Courageous, I think we can survive one day without you.

Back from the dead.

All I can tell you is do not look in your inbox.

Welcome back, I don't know how we managed without you.

Don't worry—we saved all your work for you.

I'm going to have to see a note from your doctor.

I see the tests came back negative.

So you can tell me—beach or mountains?

I was going to come visit you in the hospital with flowers and a clown, but then I found out you were just at home pretending to be sick.

Don't tell me what happened on *Oprah*. I Tivo the show all week and watch them all Friday night.

Did you finally beat Grand Theft Auto?

Let me guess, your Uncle Johnny Walker came to town for a visit?

You? I thought you'd been fired.

Sorry, but we all figured you finally quit, so we gave your job away.

# BEFORE A THREE-DAY WEEKEND

If we switched to that four-day work week, this would be a regular weekend.

Do you think the French get as excited about four-day weekends?

Road trip!

I may just come in on Monday...just kidding.

It's like a weekend on steroids.

See you on the other side.

Try to make good use of the time.

Finally enough time to eat, sleep *and* shower.

If we start driving now, we can make it to Alaska and back by Tuesday. Who's in?

If we start now, we can pub crawl half the city and back by Tuesday. Who's in?

Who wants to come by my house for a nonstop three-day *X-Files* marathon?

It goes without saying that tomorrow is a throwaway.

I'm more tired than when the weekend started.

I need a weekend to recover from my weekend.

The whole thing was a blur.

I'll be honest, I was bored silly yesterday.

I managed to squeeze in another seven showers.

I finally finished my novel.

I wondered why none of you were here yesterday.

It was nice throwing up on Sunday night because I was drunk and not because I was dreading coming here.

It's the damnedest thing: I got in my car on Friday, fell asleep in the parking lot and didn't wake up until five minutes ago.

This weekend was hardest on my errands. I kicked their butt.

I was hoping today would be a snow day.

I usually spend Saturday running errands and Sunday with my family, so the extra day allowed me to spend a whole day with my dolls.

# WHEN YOU'RE WORKING ON THE WEEKEND

No one tell me who wins the NASCAR race. I'm Tivo-ing it.

This is way better than hanging out with my loved ones.

It's so much quieter here on the weekends.

I won't complain about working on the weekend as long as nobody complains about my flip-flops.

It's fine. If I weren't here, I'd just be thinking about work anyway.

Do you think all the office supplies come alive and talk when we're not here?

No matter what we are in the middle of, one minute before the kick off of the Bears game, I'm popping open a six pack.

So this means we get off Monday and Tuesday, right?

It's a good excuse for not going to the gym, though.

# ON A TUESDAY, WEDNESDAY AND THURSDAY

## TUESDAY
Happy Almost Hump Day!

Sure beats Monday.

If today is Tuesday, why isn't tomorrow Threesday?

And I'm still hung over from the weekend.

## WEDNESDAY
Happy Hump Day!

## THURSDAY
Happy Post-Hump Day!

Can we just fast forward to Friday?

If we changed to that new four-day work week, today would be Friday.

Do you think the French get as excited about Thursdays?

# "YOU GOING TO THE OFFICE PARTY?"

Do I have to?

Is it graded?

Is there any chance it'll be canceled?

They're not paying me enough so I make it up in liquor.

Let's both go for five minutes.

Let me consult courtofopinion.com and get back to you.

I'm gonna stop in, fill a garbage bag with free chips, and head for the exit.

Only to see who does coke in the bathroom.

Not if I can help it.

Will they be taking attendance?

Oh dear me, no.

I can't. I'm allergic to coleslaw.

Yes, and I'm bringing a beer bong as a date.

Do you think work people will be there?

Only to get material for my novel.

I spent twenty minutes this morning choosing between pleated and flat-front khakis.

Wow. I feel so much more unprofessional.

If this were really "casual" Friday, I'd be in ketchup-stained sweat pants and a Metallica T-shirt.

If you think about it, Casual Friday is a bit of a misnomer. If you think about it, it's not all that "casual" nor all that "Friday." Just—please—think about it.

The nice part about Casual Friday is that it forced me to spend a lot of money on business-casual clothing that I would never have bought otherwise.

Sure, I might be casual in my choice of slacks and loafers, but I will never be casual in my attitude toward my work.

Ever since they introduced Casual Friday to the office, morale has just skyrocketed. Literally skyrocketed into outer space, where it ran out of fuel and died for lack of oxygen.

Did you know they started Casual Friday in Rome just before the Empire fell?

Things are so casual around here today that I may leg wrestle the boss.

It's times like these I really wish I had joined the Forest Service.

Is it too late to call in sick?

I really need to go outside. I'm vitamin D deficient.

I checked online, and apparently the sky is a beautiful blue today.

You know what we could really use around here? A retractable roof.

Anyone wanna roll the copier out to the parking lot?

It's OK. I forgot my sunscreen anyway.

I think nature is just taunting us now.

Can you quit for just one day?

Fresh air is for sissies. Give me stale office air any day.

This is why plants always take landscaping jobs.

Wanna make a break for it?

Let's close the shades and turn on the lights.

Yet we never hear anyone complain about how dry it is in here when it's raining outside.

# "WANNA COME TO A DINNER PARTY AT OUR PLACE?"

Unfortunately, I'm out of town right now.

I have to be home before sundown because it's Loshakippalent. It's very important to my people.

I'd have to find a dogsitter and shower and it'd be a mess and you don't want me.

With all my food allergies I just can't risk it.

Where do I send my very strict dietary requirements?

My Netflix is really backed up so I need to watch them all to be sure I get my money's worth.

I bought a twelve-pack of chicken breasts and they're gonna turn any day now, so yeah, not right now.

Is "dinner party" slang for "tons of blow"?

Only if you let me make my mother's world-famous elephant-tusk soup.

Sure, but just so you know, I always eat with my shirt off and my pants down.

Can't. Agoraphobia.

# ON THE RARE OCCASION
# THAT YOU WORK OUTSIDE

Sure beats working indoors.

I need to remember to write off my sunscreen next year.

So this is what fresh air tastes like.

This is what it's like to be a lumberjack.

Reminds me of those summers I spent working for the city parks department.

Doesn't it seem odd that people from the Netherlands are called Dutch?

How do I turn on the external air conditioning?

I'm melting.

We should bring our desks out here.

# BEFORE YOU LEAVE ON A VACATION

I wish I could take you all with me.

Don't screw this whole thing up while I'm gone.

If you need to contact me while I'm gone, please don't hesitate to write me a letter.

I don't want to tell everyone where I'm going but it rhymes with Hawaii. OK, it's Hawaii.

Don't worry, I'll take plenty of pictures.

How are you going to survive without me?

I don't want anyone touching my stuff. You listening to me over there in accounting?

If I don't come back I want you all to feel free to take any of my office supplies.

I'm going to need everyone's T-shirt size.

Well, it's better than the alternative.

Just don't make me give a speech.

Another year, another victory in the war against childhood obesity.

Where's my sheet cake?

Sure was nice of management to send me that big gift basket.

Who wants to meet me at Denny's? I'm going for lunch and dinner.

I'd love to leverage this into a day off.

I'll probably spend today like I spend all my birthdays: drunk in the bathtub.

I can't believe you all remembered and all I had to do was constantly mention for the past three weeks that I had a birthday coming up.

For the love of everything, no singing.

I'm ready to go ho, ho, home.

This Christmas I'm asking for world peace and a Flowbee.

Is the boss going to be around the next few weeks or is he too busy with his work as Ebeneezer Scrooge?

I'm all nogged up right now.

Do slippers make a good Christmas gift?

I know it's the holidays right now, but when is Christmas?

I'm going to jingle all the way home tonight.

Who is this Carol everyone keeps talking about? I don't know anyone at the company named Carol.

I have to buy a tree this weekend.

This year, I'm thankful for Zocor.

Don't forget to eat till it hurts.

Anyone else planning an all-tofu Thanksgiving dinner?

I'm thankful I get to work with all of you.

Every year, I try to eat my age in plates of food.

The only real cranberry sauce is the cranberry sauce from a can.

I'm thankful that I don't have to go to work on Thanksgiving.

I'll tell you who isn't thankful is the turkey. Think about it. The turkey gets eaten.

Happy Stuffing Day.

Raise your hand if you still have leftovers!

I don't know who got more stuffed—me or the turkey.

Why do I have the feeling my wife packed me a turkey sandwich for lunch?

This is the year I win the battle of the bulge.

I've got a bunch of left over egg nog in my car, who wants some?

I can't go to New Year's parties because of my severe champagne allergy.

I can't wait to sing the song about old somethings being forgot and something something something.

Happy New Year! We're all one year closer to retirement!

I'm on the Coptic calendar and I resent your wishes of a happy New Year.

Happy MMIX. (MMX, MMXI...)

# POWER PHRASES

## WHAT IN THE NAME OF ___ IS GOING ON IN HERE?

What in the name of profit margins is going on in here?

What in the name of carpet cleaning is going on in here?

What in the name of conference calling is going on in here?

What in the name of securities regulation is going on in here?

What in the name of refrigerator repair is going on in here?

What in the name of janitorial work is going on in here?

What in the name of outside sales is going on in here?

# CHAPTER 9
# OH, THE PLACES YOU WILL WORK

# WHEN YOU WORK IN A BANK

Say what you want—this sure beats working in a bank.

Someone remember to count the money today?

Let's hope we don't run out of nickels.

Do we get in trouble if we give people their withdrawals in two dollar bills?

Today's the day we get robbed. I can feel it.

You know what they say about banking, this is where the money is.

I'm banking on the fact that we're going to have a great day.

There's the money man.

I have a great amount of interest in the banking field.

I feel like we'd really ramp up our business if we got back into giving out toasters.

Ever feel like your life needs a little change?

It's only a matter of time till the ATM's take over.

Where do we keep the bills with the explosive ink for when we get robbed?

Hello, fellow money handlers.

Any robberies today?

What's the current interest rate?

Interest is weird, right? I mean, should we be giving people money for holding onto their money for them? I really should have taken finance.

Can you cover my counter? I need to make a deposit, if you know what I mean.

It would be great if they gave us a 20 percent discount on money.

It's strange to look at people's bank accounts. It's almost like being a doctor or something.

With each deposit, we build people's dreams.

Let's really push people on the noninterest-bearing checking accounts.

Did you know that at this branch alone we have over eight trillion dollars in deposits? No kidding.

I'm gonna take my lunch break now—and you can take that to the bank.

We appreciate your business—and you can take that to the bank.

Our thirteen-month CDs are very popular—and you can take that to the bank.

I just love saying, "No, we can't do that."

Paper or plastic?

The line forms at the bank down the street.

You can bank on that.

Who is on the one dollar bill again?

# "WANNA COME TO MY KID'S BIRTHDAY PARTY?"

I'd love to, but there are just too many bad memories.

Small people frighten me.

The old lady and I have been trying with no luck yet. Just seeing all those little faces...it would be too painful.

I don't do the whole "kids" thing.

Is there gonna be ice cream cake?

Only if there's gonna be a clown. I love clowns, especially when you can make them cry. It's like watching irony unfold before your eyes.

Sure. But instead of a birthday party, let's call it "A Salute To An Already Overpopulated Planet."

The court order says I won't be able to make it.

I don't do well with kids when I'm drunk, and if it's during the weekend, I'm gonna be drunk.

What kind of cake are you getting? I can't have anything other than white chocolate.

Is that how you think of me? As a child?

When do I get to find out what's in the secret sauce?

Stay away from the cooks. Cooks are always insane.

Any grease fires today?

So I guess this is what they called the service economy.

I'm not gonna lie—it's hard to support a heavy drug habit on tips.

The best part of this job is that people come hungry and leave happy.

I wouldn't mind getting a different crowd of regulars. The ones we got are boring.

Have you tried the new artichoke dip? It's actually pretty good.

Is that hand-washing-after-the-bathroom sign for real?

You guys all report your tips on your taxes, right?

Just one more time: forks are the pointy ones and spoons are the round ones?

What do you recommend today?

I really wish that one day we'd just run out of food and we could all go home early.

Ka-ching!

We're really on the front lines of commerce!

I'm gonna need a price check on Buckets of Fun!

Take a penny, leave a penny? I think I'll take one, thanks.

I feel like we should have an option besides just paper and plastic. Maybe wood. Or iron. Something that could also be used a weapon.

Would a tip jar really be the end of the world here?

I always consider each customer a gift.

I try not to think about all the germs that are definitely on the bills people give us.

Let's hope we get some Canadian money today.

I feel a little "checked out" today.

I'm really building up my forearm muscles using the scanner.

One of these days, I'm gonna get the count right on my register. I just know it.

I'm good with credit cards, but checks I always struggle with.

How's it going in the teeth business?

Any good cleanings coming up?

I think I read somewhere that dentists are supposed to have the highest rates of suicide. Just FYI.

Don't forget to tell people to floss.

What are we gonna do when people finally realize that they haven't really needed teeth since the invention of the smoothie?

I think we should surprise every patient we have to put under for a procedure with a new set of veneers.

If you enter the Dental Hall Of Fame, do you get a plaque?

I love this job, but sometimes I think I'm just scraping by.

If the country gets nationalized healthcare, does that cover us too or can we keep charging $4,000 for braces?

I've been watching some specials on the British royal family, and I noticed their teeth. That could be a huge market for us if you think about it.

Having thirty-two teeth is so overrated.

## MEANINGLESS ANSWERS TO COWORKERS' QUESTIONS

## "WHAT ARE YOU DOING TONIGHT?"

Not sure, but tears and Häagen-Dazs will probably be heavily involved.

Whatever my parole officer lets me get away with!

I got some sittin' penciled in for a few hours.

I'm hosting a dance party.

Probably inventing something.

Going through your garbage.

Knocking out a wall and starting some renovations.

I'm building a spaceship in my barn.

Not much if I'm fortunate.

Tonight is Me Night.

If I don't get some TV in me soon, then—watch out—because I am gonna flip out.

Helping a friend move.

I got my professional wrestling gig tonight.

The secret club I'm in has a meeting tonight.

Calligraphy class.

# WHEN YOU'RE A NURSE OR DOCTOR

Greetings, happy healers!

I like this job because I know I can find work no matter where I choose to live.

I believe in a holistic approach to treating patients.

When are we getting more free drug samples?

This is one job where it's totally cool to come to work sick. In fact, they prefer it.

Every time I meet a new patient—no matter what they're here for—I say, "Don't worry, I'm going to save your baby." They like that.

I really like it when the cute drug reps come in and flirt with us and pretend to know what they're talking about.

If this is such a great job, why is there a shortage of us?

I'm really stressed. Anyone got the key to the medicine closet?

After work I'm gonna stay at work and get a check up.

Anyone else take naps in the operating room?

Just your average night in the ER.

Can you call my cell phone? I think I left it in that guy's chest cavity.

You know how they say every second counts? But what if some of them don't count?

You know, the first two letters in "error" are E and R.

Let's save someone's life tonight.

I think we should be closed on Sundays.

Don't forget to wash your hands. This place is a giant, walk-in Petri dish.

Let's do the triage in reverse. Just for today.

What is that?

I really hope I don't see any blood today. It just makes me sick.

I really hope I get to see something gross.

Can we just shut the ER down for an hour and do a little housekeeping?

Fun to be here again amongst tragedy.

Why do we always get the sick people?

Give me your poor, your sick, your huddled masses yearning to breathe germs on me.

What a great business model we have: the vast majority of people in the waiting room don't have actual emergencies or health insurance, but we're still required by law to treat them, even if we never get paid. What a gig.

Ever feel, like, what's the point?

Where does the emergency room go if it has an emergency?

I should have gone into radiology.

I checked the waiting room and the most recent magazine we have in there is from 32 years ago.

Given the three hour wait to see a doctor, I hope nobody here has an actual emergency.

Sure does smell like a hospital in here.

I'm gonna order a pizza.

## MEANINGLESS ANSWERS TO COWORKERS' QUESTIONS

## "HOW'S THE FAMILY?"

I don't even know.

Weird.

Therapy. Lots and lots of therapy.

You're the closest thing I got to family.

I'd tell you but the judge has me under a gag order.

I wish I knew. I'm here so much.

Let's just say that there was an incident.

Do you mean my regular family or my crime family?

I think my wife may be trying to poison me.

Great. I'll send you our most recent newsletter. It's got all the updates.

Turns out they're not my real family.

My mom's side or the criminal side?

Personally, I don't much know, but they are doing the right thing and going green.

Well, I just did an hour with my therapist on the family, and even he got pretty bummed out.

This sure is great, right?

Um, this totally rules, right?

Did they give you your own sneaker yet?

Who are you gonna leave tickets for tonight?

Let's try to stay focused on the fundamentals.

Let's just take it one game at a time.

Let's always try to be winners—not just in this game, but also in the game of life.

I saw something on the news last night that apparently there's people who make less than a million dollars a year. A lot less.

Who is the Gipper, anyway? And why are we winning one for him?

What's the coach's name again?

I may have a concussion—but by any chance is my name Susan?

Do you have change for a million dollar bill?

How much is your rookie card worth?

When you retire are you gonna announce or coach?

It's all about having fun, only with a ton of money.

I don't even know what this mink coat is made from, but it sure is warm.

My goal isn't to win all the time, but to display good sportsmanship.

Don't forget to practice!

I say we *assume* it's time for lunch—who's with me?

What's the opportunity cost of going on a coffee run?

I wish the market would figure out a way to put more paper in the office printer.

The demand curve goes down, right?

I'm gonna trickle down to the candy machine and get a snack.

The big picture is out of focus.

I'm jonesing for a macro lunch.

Anyone who had predicted the meltdown of the subprime mortgage market and the collapse of the financial system would be sitting pretty right now. Man, we suck.

We should probably go answer some of our fan mail. No, I'm just kidding.

I'll tell you who's to blame for everything—the corporations. Think about it, man. Just think about it. It helps if you're stoned and don't know anything.

Remember: no eye gouges or punches to the groin.

Personally, I like the second law of thermodynamics best because it touches upon the relentless increase in entropy, or disorder, which to me is a good lens through which to view many aspects of life, history, and sociology.

Have you ever built a Carnot engine for fun?

Do you use Fahrenheit, Celsius or Kelvin?

Our nation really needs to graduate more engineers and scientists if we want to stay competitive in the global economy.

I spend way too much time thinking about the dual wave-particle nature of light.

What's that old joke about the engineer, the chemist and the economist?

Let's drop what we're doing and build a perpetual motion machine.

We can put a man on the moon but we can't make a car that does laundry. What's that about?

I should have gone into electrical engineering, but I got caught up in the mechanical engineering craze of the late 1990s.

I'm still not sold on the metric system.

# "HOW DO YOU LIKE MY TIE?"

Best tie in years.

It's rare that a man has subtly perfect taste.

Is that a math proof written on there?

There's another one that I love, so I guess it's a tie!

It's good to learn from mistakes.

It brings back fond memories. It reminds me of my grandma's old drapes.

Never seen one like it.

Didn't I see that at an antique shop?

Like as a friend or from an aesthetic standpoint?

It's a clear reminder that there's no accounting for taste.

Why, have you overheard everyone gossiping about how awful it is?

It's unfair to wear such an awesome tie and then show it off like that.

Does it know any tricks?

Love the tie, love the knot—love it all.

Are these tights slimming?

What do you hate more, death rays or kryptonite?

It's not like we're saving the world here...oh wait.

Have you lifted up one of those Hummers yet? They're heavy.

For a group of masked avengers who save the world on a regular basis, we sure do have a bad pension plan.

With the price of gas these days I sure am glad that I can fly to work.

You ever wish you had a better supervillian? Like someone who was more of a challenge?

Sometimes I think Superman is looking through my suit with that x-ray vision of his.

One of us has got to tell the Flash to wash that suit. It's getting a little ripe.

You have a hard time dating too?

I'm not kidding, I bet half those compartments on Batman's belt are completely empty.

OK you take your mask off first, and then I will.

# WHEN YOU'RE A REPORTER AT A NEWSPAPER OR MAGAZINE

Who's got the big scoop?

What has to happen to stop the presses around here?

If anyone needs me, I'll be in the kitchen covering the leftover spaghetti beat.

Extra! Extra! We're about to lose our jobs thanks to the Internet.

Here's an exclusive: I need a drink.

With a couple of tweaks, this could get you a Pulitzer.

Let's make an effort to cover up our obvious bias this week.

I think we should do more stories about how I need a raise.

This piece really sings.

I write only in the Wingdings font.

Great typesetting in this issue.

When I'm filing a story, I try to remember that truth is what I think I decide it is.

I have gotta learn to type.

Can you help me make up a few quotes?

I'd like to go follow up on a lead in my bed.

Do you wanna just pin it on someone and get out of here early?

Let's think for second: what would TJ Hooker do?

If I don't shoot somebody soon I'm gonna go crazy.

What do you say we go stake out that new record store for a few minutes?

Let's just arrest everyone and work backward.

Wanna blow off the community relations workshop and just hit the gun range?

How many guns do you carry in total?

If someone really wanted to be entrepreneurial they'd open a donut shop in the police station.

I just need one more domestic dispute and I get a free toaster.

I'll be honest—I don't even load my gun. Just to be safe.

This is the last time I choose a career based on David Milch shows.

Is it cool if you ride in the back? I want people to think I got a big collar.

# WHEN YOU WORK FOR JIM CRAMER

I'm gonna go grab lunch—BOO-YA!

Jim sure does throw a lot of chairs.

Does Jim seem stressed out sometimes to you?

I wonder if Oprah throws things a lot too.

Has Jim had his blood pressure checked recently?

I think we should call it "Angry Money."

I'm gonna start calling him Jimmy and see what happens.

I'm thinking about wearing my sleeves rolled up and my tie loosened. Do you think Cramer will notice?

Jim is in the bathroom ripping hand dryers off the wall.

You know when Jim gets really calm and says something that seems really thoughtful and rational? That's when I get scared the most.

I wonder if Jim's ever, you know, thought about talking to someone.

Anyone see Cramer? I checked his office, but all that's in there is a copy of *Crime & Punishment* and a fire extinguisher.

# "YOU SEEM PREOCCUPIED."

You have no idea.

It's a whole big thing.

Gotta meet the quarterly numbers.

The IRS found my offshore accounts again.

Just trying to figure out *The Crying Game*.

Perhaps we'll never know.

Is it that obvious? I'm trying to figure out how to tell you I love you.

Oh, family stuff. I'm suing my parents. Long story.

I have to concentrate so I don't start sobbing.

I was thinking about sharks.

Just wondering what everyone in China is up to.

I'm in sleep mode.

I'm doing my taxes.

Oh, my goldfish is sick.

I'm just worried about the whole entire world.

I'm trying to grasp the dual wave-particle nature of light.

# WHEN YOU'RE A LAWYER

You're on a short leash, counselor.

What's up, Ironsides!

I object! To how nicely dressed you are today.

You're such a great lawyer that it should be illegal.

You're totally law-some.

I was out late last night taking the "bar exam" if you know what I mean.

If you ever need a lawyer, here's my card.

What do you call ten thousand of us at the bottom of the ocean?

Just for kicks, let's find somebody on the street today and sue the heck out of them.

That outfit is so sharp you're going to have to file a "class action" suit against yourself.

I don't know, I just feel like we all dress like a bunch of lawyers.

How are we helping society again?

# WHEN YOU'RE A COMMERCIAL PILOT

Let's try to shortcut.

Wanna see how long we can go not talking to each other?

I easily could have landed that plane on the Hudson.

Arm the warhead.

We've got a couple bogies on our tail.

I've got an idea—let's buzz the tower.

You know what my favorite movie is? *Airplane*. No kidding.

I'd do this job just for the free peanuts.

Hey, we're approaching Vegas. I think we better land to check out some mechanical issues. Wink, wink.

Do you mind if I open the window? I'd like a little breeze in here.

Time for my famous barrel roll.

Let's have a freestyle rap contest on the PA system.

What do you think the flight attendants are cooking up for dinner?

Did you bring any CDs with you?

Did we forget anyone?

Who brought the booze?

Did we double check to make sure someone packed the drink carts?

The guy in 36E is crushing the people in 36D and F.

Man, where are all these people going?

Does it seem weird to you that this thing can fly with all these people and gadgets on board?

Every time we take off, I think to myself, "Thank you, Daniel Bernoulli."

I can't believe these people actually believe that the seat is a flotation device.

After we do beverage service, we should follow it up with deodorant service for the guy in 20A.

They really gotta start letting people smoke on airplanes again. It would really help pass the time.

Tell me again why we're not allowed to hang out in the cargo hold?

# WHEN YOU'RE AN AIR TRAFFIC CONTROLLER

Let's push some tin today.

I heard there's a shortage of air traffic controllers. So maybe now's a good time to ask for a raise.

Ever just have a total brain fart and forget what you're supposed to be doing?

One, two, three, four, I predict a thumb war.

Can I go home now?

Are we there yet?

Who's up for a game of chicken?

It's easy to forget, but what we do matters.

Sometimes after my shift I like to walk down to the gate and greet passengers coming off a plane and say, "Hey, just so you know, I got you here safe."

Would a cat nap hurt anything?

I keep thinking that if I stare at the monitor long enough it'll start making sense.

I'm gonna have flight 410 buzz the tower.

Each time a plane lands, I get that much closer to retirement.

# "ARE YOU GOING FOR THAT PROMOTION?"

Only if the company demands I do.

I guess we'll let the voters decide.

Everyone says I should, but I don't know.

Why not? It's free, right?

Just try to stop me!

Wouldn't you like to know.

Not if you are.

Maybe I is, and maybe I isn't.

Who wants to know?

Or is that promotion going for me?

I first need to talk to my family, my lawyer and my mistress.

Little old me?

Legally I'm forbidden from having any kind of power.

This job isn't easy, but the pay more than makes up for it.

Mold any young minds today?

You go to the union meeting last week?

Ever give detention just for kicks?

Another day and still not a single apple on my desk.

I mean, I know we all complain all the time, but going home at 3 o'clock and getting the summers off sure is hard to beat.

I gotta tell ya, I am hammered.

I may be the teacher, but I learn so much from those kids every day.

Once I get tenure, you're all gonna pay.

Let's just hope they never do away with summer vacations.

I'm so sick of hearing about how the children are the future. What about my future?

If I weren't teaching, I'd definitely be doing something equally important.

I really enjoyed my job until they started cracking down on kickball time.

Explain to me again why we're opposed to school vouchers?

The good thing is we got this union that politicians are scared of.

We should start going to the union meetings. I hear there's some interesting contract stuff going on right now.

With these kids today, we're screwed. Time to start learning Mandarin.

What was I planning on doing with my life again?

I'm still waiting for my apple.

# WHEN YOU'RE A PRESIDENTIAL CABINET SECRETARY

Even though they call us "secretaries" we don't have to take notes and stuff, do we?

Shotgun seat-next-to-the-President next cabinet meeting!

If I'm the secretary, what do I call my secretary?

Not sure about you, but I'm totally gonna run my department straight into the ground.

Before we get going, what's the official policy on graft?

That Treasury Secretary thinks he's such hot stuff.

The Secretary of the Interior better watch his mouth or he's gonna get a face full of my fist.

Does the White House validate?

Does it even matter if I don't go into the office? I mean, I'm in charge of Health and Human Services—who cares?

Before I took this appointment, I made them throw in season tickets to the Nationals.

Do we get presents on Secretary's Day?

I don't know how I got this job. My daddy just wrote a check and told me to show up here.

Let's go hand out some D's.

Let's get down and dirty.

Don't worry—I'm tough but fair.

I think those are rat feces, but my friend Benjamin Franklin would know for sure.

Let's hope you *mold* your own in this inspection.

I just hope we never have to do an inspection on my apartment. Let's just say that I doubt I'd get much higher than a C+.

What's to stop someone from just printing up their own grade? Nothing—that's what I say.

What gives us the right to pass judgment on someone else's cleanliness? I mean, why are we so special?

Do you wear your rubber gloves into the restaurant or do you put them on once you're there?

Remind me to load up on Purell.

Hairnets, hairnets, hairnets!

# WHEN YOU'RE A HEALTH INSPECTOR

Let's hope we can confiscate some questionable lobster from this place.

OK. Let's go pretend like we care.

I say we make today the day we start taking bribes.

How long till our jobs get outsourced?

In my experience, cheese can never really go bad.

## "HAVE YOU TRIED OUT THAT NEW RESTAURANT?"

Keep meaning to.

I'm allergic to that type of food.

I sort of hate new things.

Which one? The foreign one?

Do they have a lunch buffet? Because if they do, then sign me up!

I actually don't eat.

Maybe when I'm not swamped with doing these quarterly reports.

I looked at the menu and nothing sparked my interest.

Not since the health inspector failed them.

As big a priority as trying out new restaurants usually is for me, I still haven't made time to get to that one.

I tried to get a reservation, but they told me they don't serve Dutch people.

You don't know? I've been eating only Big Macs three times a day for the last nine years.

# WHEN YOU'RE WORKING ON A POLITICAL CAMPAIGN

Isn't democracy grand?

I think we should run on the issues and nothing more.

Time to go negative.

My favorite part of the day is phone banking.

Are the poll numbers in?

This is good and all, but what I really want to do is get into punditry.

Win and it's cabinet posts for everyone!

Let's start spreading rumors that our candidate and our opponent are actually the same person. I'm not sure how this will help, but it might.

I do most of my phone banking drunk. I find it helps the conversation flow a little better.

Our opponent is running under the theme of reform and fighting for the people. So we're opposed to that, right?

Did you remember to register to vote? I blanked again.

We should lie to everyone on the other side that election day is actually a week later.

Boy, women sure do love us.

I have a confession. I have no idea how to make chili.

Do you smell something burning?

I like to think of a fire as a woman—a really hot woman who burns down buildings.

It's getting hot in here!

We slide down that pole, we have huge hoses; it's all more innuendo than I can handle.

Hey, let's make a shirtless calendar for charity.

You're not a real fireman until you have a moustache.

I became a firefighter because I felt like it was time for someone to take a stand against fire.

Sometimes I wonder if all our aggressive firefighting is just creating more fires than we're stopping.

How come I never get to drive the fire truck?

I can't wait till we get to remove a giant fat guy from his house again.

Sometimes I wish 911 had never been invented.

# WHEN YOU'RE A PARAMEDIC OR AN EMT

Clear! This coffee is hot.

Clear! These shoes are new.

Clear! Let's figure out what we're doing for lunch.

Clear! Shift's over.

My favorite part is the siren and the lights. Just makes the day fly by.

Is it against the rules to use the lights to move ahead in the drive-thru line?

I became a paramedic mostly so I know help is close by when I need it.

Wanna just turn off the radio and go to the beach?

We should put a battering ram on the front of the ambulance. I bet people'd move their cars faster.

I don't care, I'm just not gonna do mouth-to-mouth on someone with bad breath. That's my breaking point.

Wanna bust out the oxygen tanks?

Do you mind if I take the gurney home with me? My bed got stolen.

Whoops.

I bet we'll get in trouble for this.

That totally looked like a gun.

But just think how much worse things could be.

It's not your fault—you have bad eyesight, right?

Looks like we're about to be neck deep in paperwork.

Well, it's back to a desk job for me.

And I just got my gun back.

Well, we all make mistakes.

I won't say anything if you buy me a bear claw and a large coffee.

What's important is—did you learn something from this?

Are you OK with me putting in for a transfer?

Where's Vic Mackey when you need him?

# MEANINGLESS ANSWERS TO COWORKERS' QUESTIONS

## "WHAT DO YOU THINK?"

Oh, that's way above my pay grade.

I haven't done that in years.

No one has ever asked me that before.

I think it's important to learn from our mistakes.

I think that history is essentially tragic. You?

That some day we're all gonna end up working for you.

I think we are all but actors, and all the world's a stage.

I think I'll have to get back to you on that one.

I don't think. I feel.

I think there's a lot of good stuff here.

I think this is your decision.

I think I'm in love.

I'm thinking about how I get out of this question.

What I always think: Let's dance!

What do I think? What do I think? Seriously? You're really asking me what I think? Hold on, my phone is ringing.

# WHEN YOU'RE A LOCAL NEWS ANCHOR/REPORTER

Any cute puppy stories in the hopper?

Let's follow this City Hall bribery story up with a cute puppy story.

Who writes these transitions for us? I mean, we sound like we're actually trying to be corny.

My favorite part is when we toss to weather.

I can't wait till we do our fake laughs with each other.

Is it OK for me to smoke on camera?

Can we get longer commercial breaks?

Whenever I interview a city official, I always want to say, "And is the ugly wardrobe standard or what?"

Can't we just get a green screen and save ourselves the hassle of driving all over the city to do live spots?

Which local news reporter is going home to cry himself to sleep? Find out at 11.

Can I say "no pun intended" when I purposely wrote the pun into my script?

# WHEN YOU WORK FOR OPRAH

Is Oprah coming in today?

We should do another one of those "Oprah's Favorite Things" shows. The audience goes nuts over that.

You think Oprah is a billionaire?

If just one person finds some healing, then I think we've done our jobs.

Ever think we should add a bubble machine to the set?

I don't think of this as a job—I think of it as a mission.

Which of Oprah's magical powers is your favorite? And least favorite?

I'll tell you this much—I've never seen Stedman in person.

It's "Secret" time.

You know what *my* favorite thing is? Fridays!

I heard if you work here for 10 years you get to touch Oprah.

One day we should do a "Things Oprah Hates A Lot" special.

I don't know how Oprah's able to be in Washington, D.C. to sign a bill into law and still make back here in time to tape a show. It's really incredible.

# WHEN YOU WORK FOR DONALD TRUMP

Let's check and see what The Donald says.

It's like we're *all* the Apprentice.

Twenty bucks to tug the hair.

I like it when he scowls.

Say what they want, but the man has got some hot lips.

What's the deal with him and gold? Everything has to be gold with him. I just don't get it.

He's just so convincing when he talks about business.

Mr. Trump is proof that if you work hard, dream big, and are born into an incredibly rich family—you can do whatever you want.

Between me and you and the wall, sometimes I think Mr. Trump's got something of an ego.

What's up, serving wench?

Sadly, during the period in question, only a few of us would have lived this long.

Anyone got any Purell? I shook the Black Knight's hand, and I think he might have the Plague.

Let's go find Bacchus and get our hands on some of his wine.

Anyone wanna start a bread riot?

We have fun here, right?

I don't want to stray too far from historical accuracy, but I'm gonna go offer the blacksmith a mint.

My folklore and mythology degree is really paying off now!

What's a knight gotta do to score some mead around here?

I bet that a lot of knights took off their armor as soon as they got far enough away from the castle that their wench couldn't see them.

I don't know about you, but I think the feudal system worked better than it gets credit for.

# WHEN YOU'RE A CAR SALESMAN

Even I don't trust me.

Sometimes I think I've lost sight of why I got into selling cars: to get people into a new car at a good price.

You know what would be funny? If we had a lemon tree in the lobby here. Now that would be ironic.

What kind of lies do I have to tell you get you to buy this car?

Hold on. I got a fish on the line here and I need to reel 'em in.

Lost another loan to Ditech!

Let's just hope no one ever finds out the truth about leasing.

You know, the Crown Victoria was an underrated car.

Careful today. I heard a rumor that the local news is doing an undercover investigation on car dealer rip offs.

So you're looking for reliability, safety, *and* fuel economy? What is this, Sweden?

We should form a trade group and try to get this lemon law thing overturned.

I just set a company record. It's not even noon and I've already told over five hundred lies today.

## MEANINGLESS ANSWERS TO COWORKERS' QUESTIONS

# "I HAVE A FINANCIAL QUESTION FOR YOU."

Your first mistake is thinking I know anything about finances.

Oh, no problem—I watch *Mad Money* every day so I should be able to answer this.

Don't get an adjustable rate mortgage.

I keep my money in shiny trinkets.

They don't call me Lil' Trump for nothing.

Invest in T-bones. Steak prices are going through the roof.

Sure. I charge $80 an hour. I take cash or cash.

The first thing to understand is that money will buy happiness.

Take the Packers and the points.

I wouldn't if I were you.

One quarter bonds, one quarter securities, one quarter real estate, one quarter precious jewels.

Never buy a car new. Thank you.

Location, location…what's the third thing again?

Sometimes a den is only a den.

When I said this place had great natural light, that was code for "Let's go drinking!"

Have you field tested the toilet in this place yet? It's like something from the space shuttle.

No joke—one time I sold a couple on a condo with an exploded sewage pipe by referring to it as an "indoor wetland."

I find the most important qualities in a realtor are good looks, pushiness, and an ability to convey an irrational sense of urgency.

I feel like causing the complete meltdown of the banking sector has really given subprime mortgages a bad name.

I always say: they're not making any more land.

You know, people can do a lot of this stuff online now without our help at all. I hope nobody finds out.

Nothing beats the feeling of seeing a young family buying their first house from another young family who just lost it in a foreclosure because they got locked into a bad adjustable rate mortgage. Really warms the heart.

Hey, where's the stove?

And how would you like that cooked?

I can't believe people eat this stuff. *Disgusting*.

Dig in people, 'cause there ain't many fish left.

Go fugu yourself.

I think you can really taste the mercury in today's catch.

I think these diners are getting a *raw* deal.

Don't say anything, but I might have made a small mistake when I was cutting up that blowfish.

What ever happened to sandwiches?

It's a crazy world where we can charge sixteen bucks for two tiny pieces of fish on a mound of rice.

Next I'm going to learn to cook Italian.

Nothing makes me crazier than when the customers try to pronounce the Japanese names for the fish. It's like, dude, just call it eel and save us all a lot of headache and pretension, OK?

It takes me seven or eight showers just to get the smell out each night.

# WHEN YOU'RE A SUPERMODEL

What's Leo doing tonight?

I'm hungry. Wanna split a box of Tic-Tacs?

I love telling people that I can't get a date. You should see their faces.

I like how we pretend like modeling is actually really hard work. And people buy it!

Seriously, I was planning to get a PhD in physics, but then this modeling thing just fell in my lap.

It's pretty awesome being this good-looking, right?

I was *such* a nerd in high school.

Can you step outside for a minute? We want to gossip about you.

Man, am I glad that I don't have to know what it's like to not have everyone wanting to do favors for you.

Don't you just hate how the stores never carry anything in a size 0?

Hey, I see the Great Wall of China.

Remind me one more time which one is Earth and which one is the moon.

Small problem, people. My container of biting red ants is empty.

Here's an idea for an "experiment." Let's see if I can urinate in this bottle from across the ship.

When are we hooking up with the international space station? I need some Cheetos and an Arizona ice tea.

Have you heard about this new device to turn our urine into drinking water? Do we each get our own one of those or do we have to share?

I suppose I should tell you now that I sleep-float.

Remind me to send a bottle of wine to the temp agency.

I'm really hoping we get to do some experiments on the effects of weightlessness on napping.

Can we turn around a day early? I'm getting a little homesick.

Wait till my ex-girlfriend hears about this.

And...action.

What's your motivation?

Who does your headshots?

You should have little cards with your headshot on them. I've heard that how DeNiro got his start.

Your face is so expressive.

Ah, the theater.

Ever do Shakespeare in the park?

You know, President Reagan got his start as an actor.

I like acting, but I can't stand having to talk to other actors.

How long till we start talking about our careers?

What's your own personal strategy for sucking the air out of the room at any social gathering?

Let's do this next scene method-style.

What I really want to do is wait tables.

## "WHAT ARE YOU DOING THIS WEEKEND?"

I've got a "honey-do" list the length of your arm.

Just laying low till the heat's off.

You're guess is good as mine. I'll black out by 8 o'clock Friday night and probably won't sober up till Monday afternoon.

I don't like to make plans.

I got a date with my parole officer.

I got my final hair transplant treatment.

Fighting with riot police.

Playing with my model railroad.

I'm going to go off the grid.

Big bank robbery going down.

Partying. Hard.

I let my wife figure that out for me.

Spend some time with the kids. They have so much energy. It's kind of awful.

Slipping into the dark shades of my mind.

Who are you betting on?

If I weren't a jockey, I probably would have been a basketball player.

I don't think of myself as a guy on a horse—I think of myself as a smaller horse riding a normal-sized horse. I don't know, it helps.

Do you think the horses gossip about us behind our backs?

Want to go halfsies on some Skittles for dinner?

If I win today, I'm going to head over to Baby Gap and buy a new outfit.

How do you wash the smell of horse off?

Sometimes I swear the horses really only care about oats and hay and nothing else.

Just once I'd like someone to give *me* a sugar cube.

What is it with all the oats? Haven't they ever tried sushi?

How come the horses always get names like Always Double Down and Show Me The Money? What's wrong with Steve or Gary?

Hope it snows this weekend.

Don't put the plow before the truck. Wait, no.

I think today I'll push the snow into some kind of drift formation on the side of the road.

Anyone see the weather report? Is it gonna snow soon? I got kids who need braces.

Do you do what I do and blast "Enter Sandman" the whole time?

Where are you keeping all the snow you collect?

If this global warming thing is legitimate, we're screwed.

If we moved to Antarctica we could work year round.

Let's go clear the roads of moisture!

This is so strange, but I remember I took one of those career aptitude tests in high school and it said I would be best at pushing snow out of the way with a big truck.

# WHEN YOU'RE A STOCK BROKER

Buy low, sell high.

Greed is good.

Any hot stock tips?

Tips are for waiters.

Are you fee-based or commission-based?

I've got a Dow Jones for some big profits.

Let's stop kidding ourselves—the stock market makes absolutely no sense.

At this point I just try to keep my annual losses below 50 percent.

I think I'm going to put in a buy order for a couple hundred shares of Time For Lunch Corp.

I'll be honest—I don't have a clue how the stock markets works.

Did you hear what Warren Buffett had for breakfast?

If it wasn't for that bail out I would have had to sell my second beach house.

Don't forget—it's only money.

Let's go grab some pork bellies for lunch.

Do you think anyone's noticed yet that we have no idea what we're doing?

I like the look of these collateralized debt obligations. Let's put all our money there.

Think about it—mortgage-backed securities are basically insured by the Federal government. What can possibly go wrong?

I know we don't actually make anything and our greed and arrogance has plunged the world economy into a recession, but even with all that said, I love this stuff.

Are there a lot of forms to fill out to get a government bailout?

I'm getting super good at checking chemicals.

My favorite part is finding out what's caught in the filter.

We may not ever win the war on algae, but we certainly cannot afford to lose it.

I'm a lean, mean chlorine machine.

I'm not gonna lie. I love getting down into the muck and the mire.

We've got the only job that you can skim from your clients and still keep your job.

The crazy thing is, I can't even swim.

You want to know the key to long life? A tall glass of pool water every day.

I say that solar heaters are the wave of the future.

Sometimes people think that all I do is clean pools, but that's not true. I also clean hot tubs.

What's the plastic-frame glasses count for the day?

The irony is that I can't actually read.

We should really start selling books on tape. Those are much easier to get through.

If these people ever find out about TV, we're toast.

I just thought of something. These receipts make great bookmarks.

I swear, half our customers think this place is a library.

Thanks to my discount, I've nearly completed my *Sweet Valley High* collection.

How many books have you actually read and how many do you say you've read just to seem sophisticated?

I'm afraid some of our titles don't have enough pictures.

Instead of a "Staff Recommendations" display, how about a "Pretentious Books For Jerks" display?

For as bad as I am with the alphabet, it's a miracle they ever hired me.

# MEANINGLESS ANSWERS TO COWORKERS' QUESTIONS

## "WHAT'S THE PLAN?"

Well, the plan was for me to take over my dad's medical practice, but that didn't exactly pan out.

I'm going to dream about our problems tonight. When I wake up, I should have the plan all figured out.

Not sure, but as a rule, the more complicated, the better.

Right now I'm thinking we should try to shoot our way out.

I'll drug him, you plant the evidence and tomorrow Sir Bosses-A-Lot will have much bigger problems than getting this thing done on time.

I don't know how to describe it, but it glows in the dark and has a can opener attached.

Is that like "The Secret"?

I create a distraction while you make a break for it.

I was thinking we'd just charge ahead sans plan.

Plan. That's a great idea.

You don't need a plan if you have blind faith.

It's a Mexican dessert made from custard.

The plan is to procrastinate and then panic.

# WHEN YOU'RE A TRANSLATOR AT THE UNITED NATIONS

Did he say "war" or "word"?

I wish I could tell you what they just said but it was an inside joke.

Good luck today. Don't forget—one wrong interpretation and it's World War III.

To be honest, I'm just making things up most of the time.

I learned your language by watching soap operas.

I wish we could just speak the universal language of love.

Who knew that Tanzania had so much to say?

What's your favorite foreign swear word?

Blah blah blah blah. Blah blah blah. Blah.

It's nice to work somewhere where you're under absolutely no illusions that you're making a difference.

I always ask, what would Dag Hammarskjöld do?

# WHEN YOU'RE A SPY

I'm not a spy.

Nobody knows I'm a spy.

Don't tell anyone I'm a spy.

This whole "spying" thing looked much more exciting when Roger Moore was doing it.

The worst part of my job is when they ask me to find out information that they don't have. It's like, how am I supposed to do *that*?

They call me *The Spy Who Loved Me*. Apparently I'm a bit of a narcissist.

Remind me to get a safe or something to put all my secret documents in. Right now they're just lying all over *my* apartment.

I keep asking for one of those cars that can turn into a submarine, but apparently my needs aren't important.

I hope my next cover is as a food critic.

Let's literally get into gear.

Did you get a tour T-shirt yet?

Wasn't like this when I worked for Zeppelin.

You know, when it comes down to it, we're really just movers.

I don't do this job for the money or for the glory. I do it because I'm fascinated by the minutiae of logistics.

The lead singer and I just made eye contact.

There's something sticky on this amp.

I totally live for soundcheck.

Does your back ever get sore?

What city are we in?

What's Kanye freaking out about this time?

Can anyone tell me the difference between a woofer and a subwoofer, and also if we use them?

What they don't get is that we have to serve them regardless of whether they tip us or not.

Toward the end of the night I just throw whatever's closest to me in a glass with some ice and charge double.

I like watching the patrons get progressively drunker, louder and pushier. Really reaffirms my faith in humanity.

I can make any drink you can think of, so long as it's either a Jack on the rocks or a gin and tonic.

People always tell me their problems, and quite frankly I don't like it.

Sometimes I pretend to be washing a glass or counting the register when I'm actually just ignoring people who want drinks.

It is true that sometimes a wise man must be drunk to spend time with his fools.

As Benjamin Franklin said, "Beer is proof that God loves us and wants us to be happy."

# MEANINGLESS ANSWERS TO COWORKERS' QUESTIONS

## "WHAT TIME IS IT?"

Half past something.

Quarter to awesome.

Busy time.

What's it worth to you?

What are you baking?

Time to shift your way of thinking.

Time to pizarty.

I don't know exactly, but it's likely time to get funky.

Time to admit what a complete waste we've allowed our lives to become.

Time for some serious regret.

It's game time, baby.

Jocks don't wear watches.

4:38.

Time for you to get serious about saving for your future.

It's your time to shine.

Let's go kill some trees.

I killed a ton of trees today.

I'd say my favorite woods are oak, maple and spruce. Not in that order.

Have you ever heard that "Lumberjack Song"? If I ever see John Cleese, I'm going to punch him in the face.

I love the spotted owl...sandwich.

This must have sucked before chain saws.

I can't believe we actually have a co-pay with our medical plan.

Did you guys know they make paper out of this stuff?

Bring it down real slow in case there's a bird nest up there.

I love these plaid shirts.

I swear, sometimes I think I can hear the trees crying.

I got into the coffee business to better myself.

When I see the lines going outside the door, I feel like a drug dealer.

I like having a job that mixes pretension with low wages. It's really just about as hip as you can get.

So this guy asked me for a five-shot cap, and I'm like, "Dude, whoa, you're gonna have a seizure."

I like to think that I am bettering society by helping people stay awake and addicted to caffeine.

Explain to me why bartenders get bigger tips than we do?

I hung out here so much they thought I worked here, so technically I never actually got hired.

It would be very confusing to work here if you had the name Joe.

See you *latte*-r.

I just want to espresso how much I love this job.

I'm running out of superlatives.

Back to you.

I may just get drunk tonight.

One of the players just did something good.

Sports are great for their ability to distract us from our loveless marriages.

Just once, *I'd* like to shoot and score.

For the record, I'm not really a sports guy.

I miss Mike Tyson. Those were the days, right?

I'm going to take a quick nap. Wake me if there's a touchdown.

Can I call you my booth buddy?

GOOOOOAAAAAAL!

We should start betting on the games, just to keep it interesting.

Anyone see the bears? They're not in the enclosure.

We gotta sign with the chimps about throwing their feces.

You gotta admit, it'd be kind of awesome if an animal got loose. Not anything dangerous, but maybe a few monkeys or something. It'd really break up the day.

I've been thinking about inventing saddles for the giraffes. We could make a pretty penny on giraffe rides.

We'd probably get in a ton of trouble for having the elephants fight the lions, right?

Let's stay after and toss some melons into the hippos' pool and watch them go all crazy territorial.

The animals have been really good lately. Let's give them a free day.

A little pink in the middle is good for the digestive system.

I like it when people send food back. If gives me a chance to learn from my mistakes, and that's invaluable to me.

When in doubt, add more butter.

Now we're cooking with natural gas.

The great thing about this business is that in three hours, they'll all be hungry again.

I'm really into spices.

One of these days I'm going to be the Iron Chef.

I'm just trying to save up enough money so I can open up a little insurance company on the coast.

Let's fill up on loose change tonight!

Let's knock this "shift" right out of the park.

What's a better a car, a Hyundai or a Mercedes? I'm not really a "car guy."

I like to think these are all my cars and they're returning them to me.

Remember: they're not dings—they're beauty marks.

I don't expect anyone to tip me. That way I don't feel guilty about smoking in their car.

Can I get a hand? I don't know how drive a stick.

They're called "bumpers" not "don't bumpers."

Great. Another Prius.

# MEANINGLESS ANSWERS TO COWORKERS' QUESTIONS

## "YOU DOING OK?"

I'm always OK.

Straight as a curly fry.

OK as can be expected.

Doing what I need to.

Livin' it.

Who's asking and why?

I try not to think about it.

I get lonely a lot.

Hangin' tough.

Never not.

Why, so you can make me see a shrink? Is it the shrink thing again?

I'm Oll Korrect.

Super-duper amazing and special.

# WHEN YOU'RE A COMMERCIAL FISHERMAN

It was either this or the NBA, but I just love fresh fish.

Do I smell? Be honest.

A bath? What are you, some kind of Communist or something?

Why do we catch thousands of little fish? Let's just go after one *big* fish.

I'm gonna say it: I hope we catch a Great White today.

Let's name each fish as we haul it in.

Everyone keep their eyes open for pirates.

I'm just saying, we'd get a lot more done with a few grenades.

If we were real fisherman, we'd be fly-fishing.

Something smells fishy.

You guys heard fish is a good source of protein? Because it is.

I keep waiting for one of these to be a magic beanstalk.

Call me an optimist, but it really feels like our business is *growing*.

OK. All these plants look good from here.

Ever wonder if we'll run out of dirt?

Sure, it's nice to work outside. But what really excites me is getting my hands dirty.

You know what they used to use for fertilizer, right? *Ish*.

As a rule, you can never have too many vines.

Does anyone really have any idea what we're doing?

I can't believe I've managed to convince all these rich people to pay me to water their plants for them.

Call me an optimist, but it really feels like our business is *blooming*.

Here's one for you—ladybugs are actually *good* for the garden.

Remember to stretch, or you'll wind up like me.

If it wasn't for the whistle, I'd never do this job.

I'm thinking about getting a badminton team going for the school.

Never underestimate the power of the jumping jack.

I see myself as the front line in the fight against childhood obesity.

You're not allowed to quit. You can give up, but you can't quit. There's a huge difference.

I'm pretty sure fewer than half my students can actually touch their toes.

I've noticed some of the smaller kids don't like sports as much as the others.

I don't think anyone is ever too young to learn about weight training.

I must have lost two dozen assistants before I got that sawing-in-half trick down.

If only I could really pull money out of people's ears, then I'd be on to something.

I tried to saw a lady in half once, but it didn't go well, and now I mostly stick to coins behind ears and things like that.

Kids' parties are good because children are so insanely gullible.

I'm trying to figure out a way to combine my love of magic and my hobby of rabbit husbandry, but I keep coming up blank.

Want to see a card trick? Watch me pay my credit card bill.

Can I get some help from someone in the audience? I need someone to cosign on an apartment for me.

Honestly, I just started doing this to meet women. Guitar would probably have been a better choice.

Right now I'm saving up to buy a new tuxedo. This one is a bit gamey.

I prefer the term *illusionist*. It sounds fancier. Whoops, my rabbit just vomited.

Ta-da!

# MEANINGLESS ANSWERS TO COWORKERS' QUESTIONS

## "YOU NEED ANY HELP?"

You mean psychological help? Then yes.

Is this the kind of help that ends with me paying you $80 an hour?

Like plants need water.

Like cars need gas.

Help doesn't even begin to describe what I need.

You sure you want on this freight train of terribility?

Yes, but I'm too pig-headed to ask.

Like you read about.

I need IMF-level help.

Are you planning an intervention? Because I can quit cold turkey tomorrow if I want to.

I think we've moved beyond help and into repeating-a-grade territory.

Why, did you see me crying in the bathroom earlier or something? Because that was my doppelgänger.

You got my distress signal?

That Phelps is a show off.

Want to buy a medal?

Enough with the free sweat pants already.

I'm thinking of running for mayor of the Olympic Village.

I'm just going to say it, I don't like the Belgians' attitude.

I can't go out tonight. I've got Olympic fever.

Can you look at the back of my jacket and tell me what country I'm from again?

I hope I don't win the gold because I have no clue what the lyrics to the national anthem are.

Hey, don't forget: *Citius, Altius, Fortius.*

Dibs on carrying the flag!

How do I figure out the going prices for precious metals?

If I don't get some Gatorade in me soon, I'm gonna flip out.

I hope Britney has another freak out soon. I just put a down payment on a condo.

I sometimes wonder if going to journalism school was worth it.

Just think, if it weren't for the ACLU, we'd be arrested for stalking.

I hope someone famous goes into rehab soon. Gotta feed the beast.

Another dream realized.

I feel so fortunate to have found a line of work that combines my love of photojournalism with my love of stalking strangers.

Is it possible some of these celebrities actually have feelings?

Forget a thousand words—this picture is worth a thousand bucks.

Is Hasselhoff still a celebrity?

As long as someone somewhere needs to get toy out of their toilet, I'm gonna have work.

This is a bunch of ballcock.

Do I smell a little weird?

I dream about sewage.

People always say that plumbers make $80 an hour, but in truth it's barely $50 after taxes.

Stand back. I'm going in.

I've got to head to the little boys' room and "jiggle the handle," if you know what I mean.

Ladies love guys in a van.

Find any weird clogs lately?

Let's all take it easy with the sexual innuendo today.

Fair warning: I am going to bend over now.

I can't believe I get paid for this.

# WHEN YOU'RE A CROSSING GUARD

(Mumble to yourself.) Look both ways. Look both ways.

So how did you get into street crossing?

Lose any kids today?

I gotta admit, this job is kinda easy.

These orange vests aren't very slimming.

If they don't obey my sign, they get my other sign. (Give the middle finger)

I hope they never put a bridge over my corner or I'm out of a job.

I love the adrenaline rush of walking out there in the street. There's nothing like it.

We should really get sidearms.

Every day I make, like, seven or eight judgment calls, almost all of them about when it is a good time to cross.

Hustle, kids!

## MEANINGLESS ANSWERS TO COWORKERS' QUESTIONS

## "GOT ANY GOSSIP?"

Just stuff about you.

Apparently President Clinton might get impeached.

Apparently everyone's getting along perfectly and people genuinely appreciate each other.

Yeah, tons of stuff about my family.

I don't like to gossip, unless of course you have something good.

Well you didn't hear it from me, but apparently most of upper management? Vampires.

Turns out a certain someone has been stealing money from the company for years, and you'll never guess who it is. Me!

Nope, but do you want to make some stuff up with me?

I don't gossip, but that Brad, he can't keep his mouth shut. And apparently that's not the only thing he can't keep shut. The other is his fly. But again, that's Brad. I don't gossip.

Keep this quiet, but Clay Aiken? Gay.

# WHEN YOU'RE A DELIVERY PERSON

I'm the guy who makes sure everyone gets their stuff.

When it absolutely, positively has to get there most of the time.

Does this box smell like weed?

How do my legs look in these shorts?

Just once, I'd like someone to send me a package.

I always wonder if I really have the build for a delivery person or if I should go back into accounting.

Do I smell a little gamey to you?

I just got a memo from HQ. Everyone gets to take home one package tonight.

Hey, what do you do with all the packages you have left over when you've finished your run?

The worst are the people who invite you in to meet their cats.

# WHEN YOU'RE A MIXED MARTIAL ARTS FIGHTER

My face hurts.

I like to parry blows with my nose.

Man do I wish I had never won the Rhodes Scholarship.

There has to be an easier way to make a living.

I started doing this sport because I needed to be held.

Do you hear a ringing noise?

I think I could take you.

Who wants to get choked out?

Who's ready for a knee bar?

When I'm not beating up dudes, I can be found tending to my garden.

I figure I should get in on this street-fighting-for-money gig before they inevitably outlaw it.

How do we get this to the next level?

Paradigm shift happens.

That attitude right there is what's going to take this thing to the next level.

Let's not call the way you used to do things around here "wrong." Instead, let's call it "incorrect."

Let's try not to fear change—otherwise you're getting fired.

Let's just start with the firings.

When in doubt, keep talking about maximizing efficiencies.

I know that we're consultants and we consult on things, but I think I'd do better as a commander who makes commands.

What does your company do again?

I feel the need...the need to read.

I think the best part about this job is that we get to check out books for free.

I had no idea homeless people loved books so much.

That Dewey Decimal system really makes the job easy.

Someone just walked out of here with a whole bunch of books without paying for them!

We're mostly catering to the non-Internet-having crowd at this point.

I like to go over to people's houses and personally demand overdue library books.

How does the employee discount work with library books?

I may have eaten some of the microfiche by mistake.

If we don't do something about this Internet, we're all gonna be out of work.

Why haven't they released the dictionary as a book on tape yet? That would sell huge!

I always mess this up, but is the thesaurus a dinosaur?

Just to double check, a passport is a valid a form of identification, right?

It's line time.

Instead of checking everyone's IDs tonight, let's try the honor system.

I never ask for an ID from anyone who is bald. I figure if they're under 21 and bald, they deserve a drink or two.

Just for fun, no one with sneakers is getting in tonight.

Let's use our biggest muscle to solve problems tonight. That's right, I'm talking about our brains.

Let's make sure all these people come in and get drunk in an orderly fashion.

They should put a velvet rope along the border with Mexico. Problem solved.

If I had things my way, everyone would get in tonight.

If the shoe were on the other foot, would we get in here tonight?

## MEANINGLESS ANSWERS TO COWORKERS' QUESTIONS

# "WHAT'S YOUR COMMUTE LIKE?"

I don't really pay attention.

I try not to think about it.

Longer than it would be, but I gotta stop and buy drugs every morning.

Like a really annoying cousin you hate.

I just sleep in the office.

I actually jog to work.

Just like any other: three, maybe four hours.

What's a commute?

It's about 18 minutes in the morning and 16-and-a-half minutes at night.

I usually wake up at three in the morning and head into the office to work, so there's, like, no traffic.

Soul destroying. Yours?

I just threw the car in cruise control and woke up here.

Wonderful if you love listening to blather on AM radio.

Ever seen that movie *Death Race*? It's like that.

Don't forget to put on your seatbelts.

Next stop: Boringville, U.S.A.

Let's see what this old girl can do.

Let's just not talk.

Everyone here? Great. Let's get this show on the road.

Anyone got any good stories that could pass the time?

Congratulations on using public transit. It's the way to go.

If anyone's got a bottle of wine, feel free to crack it open.

Do I technically have to make all the stops?

Let's hope I don't have another flashback from my demolition-derby days.

# TO YOUR FELLOW COAUTHOR OF THIS BOOK

You're kidding me.

Well, just goes to show you.

I know, I couldn't believe they bought it either.

No, we don't have to give back the advance this time.

I'm happy that I'm finally going to get the respect of the literary community.

Yeah, that's a good one!

Well, I thought of that one already but forgot to write it down.

No, I'm not jealous.

I don't know what else to tell you.

OK, well, nice seeing you too.

# WHEN YOU'RE A WINE SOMMELIER

We can't serve this wine to people. It's over four years old.

Does this stuff have a "born-on date" on it?

Quick, which wine goes best with Starbursts?

Honestly, all of this stuff tastes the same to me.

As long as it gets them drunk, right?

Have you tried the '87 Night Train?

Excellent selection, sir. Would you like me to open the jug at the table?

I'd recommend a splash of 7-Up in that pinot noir.

Do we charge a corkage on boxed wine?

Cabernet, merlot, zinfandel or...what was the last one? Pinot something? Never heard of any of these.

Did you know that wine comes from grapes?

Watts up?

I'm amped for work today.

I'm shocked by how much I love my job.

You have to be wired a little differently to do this job.

Even though I have this great job, I've always managed to stay grounded.

I've got the power!

I charge $80 an hour. Get it? *Charge*? Hi.

If I'm wrong about this, please tell my wife and kids I love them.

Can you come here and lick this wire for me?

Don't laugh. I make more than you.

Actually, I prefer the term "electro."

## MEANINGLESS ANSWERS TO COWORKERS' QUESTIONS

# "DO YOU HAVE A MINUTE?"

For you, I have a minute and thirty seconds.

This is going to take longer than a minute, isn't it?

I'm honored that you thought of me.

For you, I always have minutes.

Not really, but hey, what's my time worth really?

Are you trying to sell me a timeshare in Boca? Because I'm not interested.

Yes. I can give you 15 seconds now and another 45 some time after lunch.

Are you going to show off your 400-meter sprint to me?

Yes. You have 47 seconds left.

Is it a card trick? I hate those.

Sure, but please make it fast. I'm late to do things that I actually care about.

Sure, but while we talk, can you help move some bags of cement into my car?

What did other people say when you asked them?

Watch out for car doors.

Bikes, walkie talkies, weed: this is the best job ever.

I hear this is how Greg Brady got his start.

Haven't these people ever heard of the fax machine?

I hope this is important. I almost got killed on the way over here.

Can't you just email a pdf of this?

Helmet...check. Livestrong bracelet...double check.

I really need to get some brakes on my bike. I don't know how many more car doors I can take.

Check out these quads.

What's in here? Lead?

Screw this, I'm taking a cab.

Let's ride!

# WHEN YOU'RE A CONSTRUCTION WORKER

My lunchbox is packed with expensive French cheeses.

You look adorable in that hard hat, Chuck.

Load-bearing, schmoad-bearing.

It's getting warm out and I'm wondering how uncomfortable you'll feel if I start wearing shorts.

I bet if we sing, the workday will just fly by.

When's the next demolition?

Before you fire up the jackhammer, I just want to tell you that I care about you.

Blueprints are just basic guidelines, right?

I'll be right back. I'm gonna go check my email.

Anyone wanna try to try that old crazy-glue-the-helmet-to-the-I-beam trick?

Safety aside, these steel-toe boots look just *fantastic*.

# WHEN YOU'RE AN AMBASSADOR

Yes! I *am* above the law!

I'm just glad I didn't get stuck with a useless country like Liechtenstein.

It's Ambassing Time.

Where'd you get those little flags for your car?

Let's leg wrestle for it.

I'm about to get all Madeleine Albright on you. Boo-ya!

We'll give you Iowa if you support our actions in the Middle East.

We have over 1000 thermonuclear missiles. Just saying.

How do you say "hello" in this stupid language?

I'm gonna need some more diplomatic immunity.

What? You guys don't fist-bump over here?

Credentials? I was the Vice President's roommate in college.

# WHEN YOU'RE A CONCIERGE

You're not leaving this nice hotel dressed like that, are you?

I would wear this hat even if they didn't make me.

Someone should do a behind-the-scenes reality show about this place. It's crazy here!

The customer is always right. Except you. You are clearly wrong.

For an extra $5 per night, I will read you a bedtime story.

Off the record? Don't go outside. This is a high-crime neighborhood.

Sorry. I no speaka your language.

Can I help you with those bags, sissy?

What do I look like, a hotel concierge?

Fire! Nah, I'm just joking. We're cool.

Ugh. You people again.

# WHEN YOU'RE
# A MAKE-UP ARTIST

Sad clown or happy clown?

Are you allergic to snake-based products?

Lunch break! We'll finish the other half of your face in an hour.

So much hair! I'm just going to do a controlled burn here.

Eyeliner is for suckers.

Be sure you wash this off as soon as you get home. It's Chinese and about 80 percent lead.

What would you like to make awkward small talk about?

If you break out into hives, don't worry. That's completely normal with these kind of chemicals.

Wow, I like this so much better than dog grooming.

# WHEN YOU'RE
# A PLASTIC SURGEON

What a mess. Now this here is precisely why I have malpractice insurance.

Wait. Why is everyone wearing gloves?

Here's that weird artery I can never pronounce.

Wires? I knew it! She's a cyborg! Run!

Trust me, I will chop off all the ugly.

This damn double vision is driving me nuts.

I went to med school in the Caribbean. It was totally awesome.

Am I supposed to be cutting out this aorta thingy?

You're not just my patient; you're my BMW 5-Series.

Why exercise for a whole year when it can be fixed in an hour of surgery?

Operating is the only thing that makes the voices go away.

I never really bought into that whole "sterile-operating-environment" deal.

## MEANINGLESS ANSWERS TO COWORKERS' QUESTIONS

## "YOU LIVE AROUND HERE?"

Wait, you mean you don't live in your cubicle?

I live in the woods.

Nearby, but also very far.

I live in a Winnebago, so I kind of live everywhere.

I'm not comfortable discussing that with people who might end up hating me.

I got a few houses in the area, one for each family.

Yup. Just up in the ceiling panels.

I actually live on another planet.

No, I live really far away. But I still walk to work.

I don't know. We should clock it with your odometer.

Never measured.

I live fifty miles north of here, but I usually just crash at my crack house, which is within walking distance.

Why are you asking me these personal questions?

I live wherever work tells me to live.

I wouldn't call what I do at night "living."

# WHEN YOU'RE A LIFE COACH

How would I know? I'm just a life coach.

Drop and give me 20 reasons why you're a winner.

Listerine is 90 percent of success.

Rub some dirt on it.

Walk it off.

Have you tried giving up?

Never forget that you are unique, if only by the definition of DNA.

Stay tuned, more from Dr. (your name) coming right up.

Try serving your emotional weaknesses to life's backhand.

Honestly, I just don't think you can do it.

Be more positive. That will be $50, please.

Pessimists are never going to do anything right.

# WHEN YOU'RE A TSA SECURITY SCREENER

Can one of you grab me some nail clippers today?

Why does it always smell like feet around here?

I have to admit, I think it's kind of funny when people make bomb jokes.

OK, now you search me.

We'd all go home with a lot more loot if we changed the rules about what's allowed more often.

Sir, please put your hands in the air like you just don't care.

Sir, I'm now going to pat you down in a way that neither one of us wants.

Hey everyone, you're all going to miss your flights because this moron packed toothpaste.

Is that a gun or a hairdryer? Oh, who cares.

Sorry. We just totally x-rayed you by accident.

Sir, we're going to have to confiscate your pants.

# WHEN YOU'RE A FARMER

This here tomato's bigger than a federal subsidy.

I'm getting sick and tired of all this dirt.

I think the Farmer's Almanac should include a list of farmers.

Yeehaw! Wait. Is that a cowboy thing?

You say potato, I say potahto. But I'm right because I'm a farmer.

I can't believe people eat this stuff.

Who's up for some hardcore farming?

Do we *really* need worms for the soil? Because...I mean...*ick*.

Don't count your chickens before they die of Asian bird flu.

I just lost my last needle in this haystack. So ironic.

Let a sleeping dog lie, or your hand will look like this.

Where's my Cat Diesel hat? I can't farm without it.

You guys wanna make small talk about crop yields?

Why do we have to start every day at the crack of dawn?

Someone's gotta keep this country obese.

## MEANINGLESS ANSWERS TO COWORKERS' QUESTIONS

## "WHERE ARE YOU FROM?"

Krypton.

I'm not really sure.

For my safety, the FBI won't let me say.

Wherever my head lands at the end of the day.

Cheyenne, Wyoming.

My daddy always said I fell straight from heaven.

Marlboro Country.

That's a little personal, don't you think?

Everywhere, yet somehow nowhere. I'm very deep and mysterious.

I actually have been meaning to find out.

I moved around a lot as a kid, ran away when I was thirteen, rode the rails for a few years, and finally settled down here on a bet with a roughneck in a card game. You?

Are you kidding me? We grew up across the street from each other. How could you forget?

I was raised in the jungle by a family of wolves and a kindly bear named Baloo.

371

# WHEN YOU'RE AN INSURANCE AGENT

How come no one calls us when they have good news?

All our products are backed by the full faith and credit of AIG.

Yeah, boyeeee!

Trust me, I could sell a refrigerator to Eskimos.

Sign here, here, here, here, and here, and initial here, here...
and here.

So much fun! I don't know why they call it paperwork.

Man, oh man, are these actuarial tables ever a bummer.

Don't bother yourself with the small print. I read it, and man,
is it boring.

I'm going to insure the bejesus out of you.

We should be OK so long as there aren't any hurricanes in the
next 25 years.

Insure. It comes from the Latin, meaning "inside sure."

# WHEN YOU'RE A COLLEGE PROFESSOR

In order to ruin the curve, I will be taking the midterm.

*Vis-à-vis, ad infinitum, non sequitur, de facto, et cetera.*

Please turn to page 134,873 in your text book.

Here's me in a fuzzy bunny suit. Next slide please.

Wait, the test should read, "Mark F if true and T if false."

I will not be answering any dumb questions this semester.

The holidays are coming up, and my book makes an excellent gift.

Look, I will not attempt to make physics interesting. That was Newton's job.

So, where's the party tonight?

A friend in tweed is a friend indeed.

Before you take tomorrow's final, please remember that I can never have too many gift certificates to the Cheesecake Factory.

# WHEN YOU'RE A MASSEUSE

I hope you like talking. I like talking.

You have some stress built up in your pancreas.

Am I rubbing you the wrong way?

Nurse, scalpel please.

What smells like feet?

How long since your last massage? You should be getting at least one per fortnight.

Prepare to be healed by the power of touch.

Anything you tell me is covered by masseuse-patient confidentiality.

Ew! Gross! Get it off!

Remember to drink lots of water so you won't die later.

You have soooo many toxins in your neck.

You know what you need? A massage...

## THERE'S NO I IN _____.

There's no I in waste management.

There's no I in Oakland A's.

There's no I in conference call.

There's no I in crane operator.

There's no I in caddy.

There's no I in DJ.

There's no I in data entry.

There's no I in weatherman.

There's no I in rodent removal.

There's no I in coauthor.

There's no I in editor.

# ABOUT THE AUTHORS

## Jacob Lentz

Jacob Lentz was born and raised in Minnesota, where he learned the value of reticence at a young age. Throughout his life, he found himself working and living in locales among people who thought not talking was "weird," so he's taught himself to fill the air with witticisms and charming nothings. Now a writer for *Jimmy Kimmel Live*, Jacob lives in Los Angeles, though he spends as much time as possible silently ice fishing in Minnesota.

## Paul Koehorst

Paul Koehorst is a TV writer and producer from Pacific Grove, California. Despite having a lackluster work ethic, he has managed to succeed in the highly competitive television industry thanks to his likable disposition, easy-going nature and inoffensive personality. A master of meaningless workplace conversation, Paul is confident that most of his coworkers would consider him a "friend" but he rarely finds himself spending any time outside of the workplace with them. He currently resides in Los Angeles and is available to play golf while training you in his methods.